# CAT'S CRADLE

## *Kurt Vonnegut*

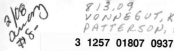

AUTHORED by Kellee Patterson
UPDATED AND REVISED by Adam Kissel

COVER DESIGN by Table XI Partners LLC
COVER PHOTO by Olivia Verma and © 2005 GradeSaver, LLC

BOOK DESIGN by Table XI Partners LLC

Published by GradeSaver LLC, www.gradesaver.com

First published in the United States of America by GradeSaver LLC. 2006

GRADESAVER, the GradeSaver logo and the phrase "Getting you the grade
since 1999" are registered trademarks of GradeSaver, LLC

ISBN 978–1–60259–066–3

Printed in the United States of America

For other products and additional information please visit
http://www.gradesaver.com

# Table of Contents

# Table of Contents

# Biography of Kurt Vonnegut (1922–2007)

One of the 20th century's great American pacifists was born on Armistice Day. Born in Indianapolis on November 11, 1922, Kurt Vonnegut entered a well–to–do family that was hit very hard by the Depression. Vonnegut went to public high school, unlike his two older siblings, and there gained early writing experience writing for the high school's daily paper. He enrolled at Cornell University in 1940 and, under pressure from his father and older brother, studied chemistry and biology. He had little real love for the subjects, and his performance was poor. He did, however, enjoy working for the *Cornell Daily Sun*. In 1942, Vonnegut left Cornell as the university was preparing to ask him to leave due to poor academic performance. He enrolled at the Carnegie Institute of Technology (now Carnegie–Mellon) in 1943. He studied there only briefly before enlisting in the U.S. Army. His mother killed herself in May 1944.

On December 14, 1944, Vonnegut was captured in the Battle of the Bulge. He was held as a POW in Dresden, a beautiful German city with no major industries or military presence. The bombing of Dresden was unexpected. Vonnegut and the other POWs were some of the only survivors. They waited out the bombing in a meat cellar deep under the slaughterhouse.

Vonnegut was repatriated in May 1945. He returned to the United States and married Jane Marie Cox. He studied anthropology at the University of Chicago, but the department unanimously rejected his M.A. thesis. (According to the university's rules, a high–quality piece of writing could be substituted for a dissertation. Twenty years later, Vonnegut showed the department Cat's Cradle, and he was given his degree in 1971.) Vonnegut worked various jobs during his time at the University of Chicago and throughout the 1950s.

Vonnegut's first short story, "Report on the Barnhouse Effect," was published in 1950. Vonnegut has expressed some dissatisfaction with his short stories, saying that he mostly wrote them for money while working on his novels, which are more important to him. But some of his stories are accomplished works in their own right, and many readers gain their first exposure to Vonnegut through these stories, which combine in condensed form Vonnegut's trademark humor, fantasy, and social commentary. Dozens of Vonnegut's short stories and two novels appeared in the 1950s.

Due to his reputation as a science fiction writer, Vonnegut's first novels were published only as paperbacks with gaudy covers that misrepresented the novels and discouraged serious critical attention. The hardcover editions of Cat's Cradle (1963) and *God Bless You, Mr. Rosewater* (1965) were a significant improvement, although they sold only a few thousand copies. In 1966–1967, all of Vonnegut's novels were reissued in paperback, and he began to develop a significant underground following.

During the 1960s, Vonnegut published a collection of short stories and four more novels, including his sixth and greatest novel, Slaughterhouse Five. The novel's popularity and broad critical acclaim focused new attention on Vonnegut's earlier work, and soon *The Sirens of Titan* sold over 200,000 copies.

He has continued to write prolifically. His most recent novel is *Timequake* (1997). His most recent book of essays is *A Man without a Country* (2005).

Vonnegut has been an important mentor for young pacifists since he began writing. His novels are known for their dark humor and playful use of science fiction, as well as their serious moral vision and cutting social commentary. Although his novels have been criticized for being too simplistic, he has a cult following of readers who love his imagination and sense of humor. He is at once irreverent and highly moral, and this rare combination has made his voice integral to American literature.

# About Cat's Cradle

Cat's Cradle, like many of Vonnegut's other novels, gets considerable mileage from irony and humor as it makes serious points about the state of the world and humanity. His tone is often light, but his words have a considerable bite. The novel is a tale of caution. Vonnegut wrote it in the wake of the Cold War and Cuban Missile Crisis, amid growing concerns about the American role in international relations and the ability of the world's greatest powers to destroy entire nations or the world with the click of a button. Cat's Cradle centers on this worry, with the main plot involving one of the developers of the atomic bomb and a deadly substance called ice–nine.

Vonnegut represents parts of his life in the novel through its characters. The family structure of the Hoenikkers is not unlike Vonnegut's, many of the characters hail from his home state of Indiana, and a few attended his alma mater, Cornell. These parallels allow the sometimes fantastical novel to be grounded in reality, creating the assumption that no matter how comical the characters may be, there are people in the world who act and think like they do. The result is a great example of the ironic, critical style that his readers love.

Throughout the novel, Vonnegut makes allusions to the Book of Jonah and Moby Dick. The novel opens with the lines, "Call me Jonah," which is a joint allusion to the opening statement of Melville's Ishmael and a biblical story of rebellion against God's will. Like Jonah of the Bible, Vonnegut's narrator will be required to follow a path that he neither wants nor understands, and his role in the events of the novel cannot be underestimated. At the end of the novel, he is one of the sole survivors, and he must tell his and the other characters' tales, much like Ishmael in Moby Dick. The dystopian world that Vonnegut creates is based on a rich literary tradition, and it is essential to his characterization of the world in which his characters and readers live.

One of the most compelling aspects of the novel is Vonnegut's distortion of the concepts of truth and lies. He warns that "Nothing in this book is true," yet the reader's historical and personal experiences make the novel's events seem real and valid. This disclosure is paralleled in the Books of Bokonon, which Bokonon repeatedly admits to be lies, but which are followed, religiously, by all of San Lorenzo's inhabitants. As the narrator of the story, Jonah is able to provide omniscient insight at different points in the story which help foreshadow certain events but also reveal the white lies and misunderstandings in which all of the characters become involved. Without Jonah to provide insight and clarification, it would not be clear who is lying or whose sense of reality is most accurate. Still, Jonah's involvement in telling the story helps highlight the fact that real life has no narrators, and what many readers might consider true in their own lives might simply not be so.

# Character List

**Newt Hoenikker**

Felix's youngest son, Newt was a midget who flunked out of medical school at Cornell. He was briefly engaged to a Russian dancer.

**Felix Hoenikker**

He won the Nobel prize in physics and was one of the fathers of the atomic bomb. The inventor of ice–nine, he left the creation to his three children Newt, Angela, and Frank. Felix was always engrossed in his work and showed little concern for his family or any other people.

**Angela Hoenikker**

Felix Hoenikker's tall, unattractive eldest child. After her mother died in childbirth with Newt, Felix withdrew Angela from school to take care of him, Frank, and Newt. Despite her unhappiness, Angela believed her father was an unappreciated saint. After her father's death, Angela traded her share of ice–nine to Harrison C. Conners, a scientist involved with top secret weapons research for the U.S. government, in return for his agreement to marry her.

**Miss Faust**

Dr. Breed's secretary.

**Emily Hoenikker**

Felix Hoenikker's wife and the mother of Newt, Angela, and Frank. She died when giving birth to Newt. Felix did not show much attention to his wife when she was alive, and her death did not seem to affect his attitude.

**Jonah**

The narrator. His given name was John, but he adopts the name Jonah in the opening lines of *Cat's Cradle*. His aspirations to write a book about the day the atomic bomb was dropped on Hiroshima, titled *The Day the World Ended*, led to his contact with Angela, Frank, and Newt Hoenikker. He became involved with their efforts to buy happiness through the use of their father Felix's scientific creation, ice–nine.

**Bokonon**

He hoped to turn the impoverished island of San Lorenzo into a utopia. After realizing the futility of his efforts, he sought to offer the people of San Lorenzo hope through the lies of his religion, Bokononism. He became a prophet to the people, but he became a fugitive on the island because of his teachings.

## Zinka

A Ukrainian ballet dancer who was briefly engaged to Newt. She was a Soviet spy who returned to her country after stealing ice–nine from Newt.

## Frank Hoenikker

The second child of Felix and Emily Hoenikker, Frank showed much of his father's lack of concern for others. After disappearing from Ilium after his father's funeral, he bought himself a job as Major General on San Lorenzo by giving ice–nine to the island's dictator.

## "Papa" Monzano

The dictator of San Lorenzo who employed Frank as Major General in exchange for ice–nine. He persecuted Bokononists for their involvement in the religion. Monzano committed suicide by swallowing ice–nine.

## Mona Monzano

The extremely beautiful adopted daughter of "Papa" Monzano. He adopted her to raise his popularity. The Books of Bokonon prophesized that Mona would marry the next President, and Mona was a devout Bokononist. Mona committed suicide by swallowing ice–nine.

## Miss Pefko

A secretary at the research laboratoy in Ilium. She expressed dismay that she did not understand any of the research that was being done at the laboratory and exemplifies the uneducated masses with respect to science.

## Marvin Breed

Asa Breed's brother, who owned and operated the tombstone shop in Ilium. He was in love with Emily Hoenikker before she met Felix.

## Dr. Breed

Dr. Asa Breed was Felix's supervisor at the research laboratory where Felix helped develop the atomic bomb. Jonah interviewed Dr. Breed for his novel, but Dr. Breed was offended by Jonah's questions because he thought Jonah believed scientists were indifferent to the plight of humanity. He told Jonah about Felix's ideas about ice–nine, but he denied that Dr. Hoenikker had been successful in creating it.

## Jack

Owner of the hobby shop where Frank Hoenikker worked in high school. He showed a lot of pride in the work that Frank produced while he worked at the show and was outwardly emotional when the subject of Frank's death was discussed.

## Sherman Krebbs

The artist whom Jonah let stay in his apartment when he traveled to Ilium. He was the wrang-wrang in Jonah's karass because by wrecking Jonah's apartment and killing his cat, he turned Jonah away from nihilism and made him a more receptive target for Bokononism.

## The Crosbys

H. Lowe and Hazel, bicycle makers whom Jonah met on the plane to San Lorenzo. They told him about the hook, a form of punishment on the island, and they gossiped that Horlick Minton was a Communist. Hazel was delighted that Jonah, Newt, and Angela were Hoosiers, because it made them members of her granfalloon.

## Horlick and Claire Minton

American ambassador to San Lorenzo and his wife, who were seatmates with Jonah on their flight to the island. They introduced Jonah to Philip Castle's novel about the island, which gave him his first exposure to Bokononism.

## Earl McCabe

The man with whom Bokonon washed up on the shores of San Lorenzo. He and Bokonon created a society of Dynamic Tension in which the religion of Bokononism was condemned to give the religious life of the people more zeal. Although he began his role as dictator in an attempt to provide hope to the people in the form of the distraction of religion, it soon became too difficult for him to maintain the behavior of an evil dictator, and he committed suicide.

## Philip Castle

Owner and manager of Casa Mona, the hotel at which Jonah stayed during his visit to San Lorenzo. He grew up with Mona as a devout Bokononist and gave Jonah some insight into the plight of the San Lorenzans and their involvement in Bokononism.

## Julian Castle

Former millionaire who built and ran the House of Hope and Mercy in the Jungle for twenty years. A devout Bokononist, he administered the last rites to San Lorenzans after they died. He taught Jonah a great deal about the practice of Bokononism on the island.

## Stanley

Frank Hoenikker's servant.

## Dr. Vox Humana

A Christian minister who studied in the States before returning to San Lorenzo. He was there to administer "Papa's" last rites, but was turned away when "Papa" revealed he was a Bokononist.

## Dr. Koenigswald

A physician who served with the S.S. in Germany for fourteen years, including six years at Auschwitz. He worked at Castle's hospital in San Lorenzo as penance for his past sins, and he was "Papa" Monzano's doctor. He administered "Papa's" last rites, according to the Books of Bokonon.

## Nestor Aamons

A Finnish architect who designed Julian Castle's charity hospital on San Lorenzo. He was Mona's biological father, and he used to live in Frank's house on Mount McCabe.

## Harrison Conners

A scientist involved in weapons research for the U.S. government who married Angela Hoenikker in exchange for a piece of ice–nine. His marriage to Angela was not happy; he cheated on her and treated her poorly.

## The Hundred Martyrs to Democracy

San Lorenzo declared war on Japan and Germany after the bombing of Pearl Harbor, and tried to send one hundred men to the States to help with the war effort. A German submarine sank the ship in San Lorenzo's harbor, killing all of the soldiers. San Lorenzo created a national holiday in their memory.

# Major Themes

### The Rejection of Truth as Innately Good

Vonnegut often juxtaposes science and religion in *Cat's Cradle*. He characterizes science as a form of discovering truth, while he characterizes religion as a form of creating lies. Despite this negative depiction of religion, Vonnegut's most severe criticisms are reserved for science and its goal of seeking and discovering truth. Vonnegut attacks the idea that truth is innately desirable and good, seeing it as a pervasive belief in our culture. He describes a realistic world in which truth is used for material and personal gain without concern for the lasting effects those truths will have on humanity.

Felix Hoenikker's invention, ice–nine, was created to address the military's need for a way to get through mud quickly while traveling in the field. Ice–nine, which effectively freezes any liquid with which it comes in contact, could be heralded as a great success for science and a considerable asset to the U.S. military. But Hoenikker also realized the extremely destructive nature of his invention, which could be used as a biological weapon to permanently destroy a nation's water supply and ensure its eventual demise. Thus, the truth that he created through science was at once a danger to humanity.

Felix and Frank Hoenikker's experiences as scientists seem to reveal that scientific knowledge does not provide sufficient answers to human problems, although many people think that it can. Science is frequently exploited to create human problems, and scientists like the Hoenikkers usually do little to prevent this result because they are too concerned with discovering truths to weigh the consequences of their discoveries.

Felix Hoenikker, sensing the gravity of his discovery, hid ice–nine from the research company for which he worked. Unfortunately, he did not have the presence of mind to realize that the remnants he left for his children to find would ultimately lead the world to the fate that he was trying to avoid, simply because his children could not resist the power that his discovery would give them. His truth led to their deaths and ultimately to the death of everyone on the planet.

### Salvation in Lies

Vonnegut presents religion as more useful and less dangerous than science, despite its paradoxes and shortcomings. In the novel, religion is beneficial not because it conveys some truth about the world, but rather because it gives people elaborate lies in which to believe. Bokonon's lies prove more liberating than the Hoenikkers' truths, because his lies have the means for making men feel better about their lack of purpose and destitute existence.

One of Bokononism's central ideas is that man has always been responsible for giving life meaning, since it inherently lacks meaning. Thus, the possibility of happiness exists in this world if only man gives life the "right" meanings. Bokononism's purpose is to provide people with better and better lies that will keep them from seeing the Hobbesian truth that life is short and brutal. It is their belief in his lies that keeps the people of San Lorenzo alive, and this creates a paradox for Bokonon. Although he is making people's lives better with his lies by giving them a reason to continue their unhappy existence, his encouraging them to continue that existence actually leads them to experience more real suffering (such as starvation and injuries). His lies are both their source of hope and the reason for their continued acceptance of their destitution, and by the end of the novel it is unclear whether he is right or wrong for propagating his lies.

Vonnegut's allusion to the Book of Jonah may provide some clarification of the paradoxical characterization of Bokonon's lies. In the biblical tale, Jonah the prophet tried to resist God's command to pass judgment on the people of Nineveh, which caused God to interfere with his life and trap him in the belly of a whale for three days. When Jonah finally conceded to God's will and was released from the whale, he did what God had commanded. Later, God saved the people of Nineveh, which made Jonah's prophecy a paradox if not a lie. But if Jonah's prophecy against Nineveh was necessary for the salvation of the people of Nineveh, then perhaps paradoxes and lies serve noble purposes. Such an argument might lend moral credence to Bokonon's approach.

## The Futility of Human Pursuits

When Julian Castle throws Newt Hoenikker's painting into the waterfall on Mount McCabe, he does so to make a point about the meaninglessness of life. Newt had painted a cat's cradle as a symbol of the pointless games that adults teach children, ascribing meaning to them when there is none. Castle took it a step further when he acknowledged that even making commentary on the meaninglessness of these activities was a waste of time, because the world does not learn or benefit from experience. When Vonnegut depicts Bokonon as a holy wanderer finding nothing but junk, lies, and idiocy, he is talking about the creations of humanity and their attempts to convince themselves and others of the importance of their pursuits. Bokonon laughs when he thinks of these fools, because human pursuits will never matter, and it will never even matter whether he laughs or cries.

## Religion and Science as Panaceas

The dichotomy between religion and science is epitomized by the opposite worlds of Ilium and San Lorenzo. The first is the setting where scientists create in a moral vacuum, while the other is a society deeply entrenched in the "foma" or untruths of a madman whose only purpose in life is give them hope. Each is the product of a separate intellectual system, but they are twin states of being because they each provide a façade with which one can obscure a horrible life. Both serve as examples to Jonah that improving the human condition is futile.

In the end, neither Ilium's science nor San Lorenzo's religion could truly save any of Vonnegut's characters from their wretched existences. The world had no real concern for their happiness. God, like many of the scientists in the novel, was interested in putting humans in interesting situations, but in the end had no emotional investment in their final plight. Bokonon writes that people should just be happy for the memories that they will bring with them when they return to the mud, because crying over one's fate is just as meaningless as laughing about it.

## The Danger of Technological Advancement

An overriding theme of the novel is that technological advancement could lead to the destruction of the human race because of science's frequent disinterest in humanity's survival. Vonnegut attempts to show that humans' temptation to control life, death, and nature has led to advances like the atomic bomb and other novel ways of bringing death in exchange for power. Scientists such as Felix Hoenikker are one of Vonnegut's primary concerns, because they seem to lack the moral capacity to care about other people. Because Felix is portrayed as somewhat childlike, there is almost the assumption that others were been more responsible for his moral transgressions than he was. Indeed, since he was a man who could become distracted by almost any toy or trick, much of the blame for his creation of deadly weapons lay on the shoulders of the politicians and government officials who filled his laboratory with materials for building weapons.

## Interpersonal Relationships

Most of the characters in the novel were involved in a number of interpersonal relationships took the form of specific groups. These "karasses" and "granfalloons" had differing degrees of importance, and because it was almost impossible for a human to know the limits of one's karass or the work it was supposed to do on Earth, many characters placed an undue amount of importance on the granfalloons in their lives. Often, Jonah would note some of the superficial characteristics he and other characters had in common, such as his and Newt's ties to Delta Upsilon. Hazel Crosby was a perfect example of humans' overemphasis on granfalloons, in that she took an unnatural pride in the number of successful Hoosiers she met.

In contrast, the Mintons never mentioned any granfalloons of which they might be members and were proud members of the only duprass in the novel. Their seeming concern with only their God–given team exempted them from the comical light in which other groups were portrayed, almost as if their perfect union exempted them from other human flaws.

## Individual Destiny and Control

The novel questions the idea of self–determination, the ability of a person to control one's individual destiny. Being reasonably able to determine one's destiny relies on the assumption that one lives in a fairly predictable, meaningful universe.

If this is not true, the events that occur are better characterized as chaotic and absurd, and people are simply creating their own meanings to mask their ignorance.

Jonah repeatedly experienced feelings that he was being compelled to do certain things or visit certain places. His always being in the right place at the right time seemed to him to be an indication that God was controlling his life and leading him to his destiny. Yet, it is unclear whether Jonah was destined to end up in a certain place simply because that just happened to be where he did end up. The idea of destiny, therefore, could be interpreted as either an unalterable series of events or the set of events that one sets in motion through one's choices. Bokonon, as a prophet, supported the idea of an unalterable destiny because he would predict the future. Even so, his predictions were often public knowledge, and it is unclear whether individuals made his predictions come true because they believed such things would come to pass and prepared the way for them to happen.

## Desire and Happiness

The theme of desire and its effect on happiness provides some of the most lugubrious if not fully tragic moments in the novel. Frank's primary desire was to create a world that he could orchestrate technically, like that of the model town he built in Ilium. He pursued this desire to the destruction of the human race, because he used his father's ice−nine to bribe "Papa" Monzano for power. Angela desired a companion after being left alone by her brothers and deceased father, but she was so desperate that she could not see that Harrison Conners was using her for her piece of ice−nine. She thus found herself stuck in a loveless marriage. Newt, likewise, was searching for love. His desire for a companion allowed him to be fooled by a Ukrainian spy into thinking that she was half her actual age and in love with him, which allowed her to steal a piece of his ice−nine.

All of the Hoenikkers were given the opportunity to make their greatest desires come true, but when they got what they asked for in some form or another, none of them became happy. The reader ends up with the suggestion that it is better to want nothing at all, as though all human pursuits really are meaningless and nothing can bring happiness.

# Glossary of Terms

**anteroom**

an outer room that leads to another room and that is often used as a waiting room

**boko–maru**

a Bokononist ritual in which individuals press the soles of their feet together to "mingle their awarenesses"; Bokononists believe that it is impossible to be sole to sole with an individual without loving that person

**Bokononism**

religion created by Bokonon, outlined in the Books of Bokonon, and practiced in the Republic of San Lorenzo

**Bokononist**

follower of the religion of Bokononism

**Borasisi**

the sun

**busy, busy, busy**

Bokononist phrase uttered in response to how unpredictable and complicated life is

**calypso**

a Bokononist poem

**cosmogony**

a theory or myth concerning the coming into existence, creation or origination of the universe

**duffle**

the destiny of thousands of people when placed in the hands of a stuppa

**duprass**

a karass made up of only two people

**Dynamic Tension**

Bokononist theory that good societies could be built only by pitting good against evil and keeping the tension between the two high at all times

**Fata Morgana**

a mirage named after Morgan le Fay, a fairy who lived at the bottom of a lake

**foma**

harmless untruths, intended to comfort simple souls

**funeral pyre**

a combustible heap for burning a dead body as a funeral rite

**granfalloon**

a proud and meaningless association of human beings; a false karass or a team that is meaningless in terms of the ways God gets things done (e.g., the Communist party, the Daughters of the American Revolution, the General Electric Company)

**hook**

the primary method of punishment in San Lorenzo; criminals were hung from the hook after being impaled through the stomach

**Hoosier**

a person from Indiana

**ice–nine**

Felix Hoenikker's creation, it can turn any liquid into a solid through a unique process of crystallization

**kan–kan**

the instrument that brings individuals into their karass

**karass**

team of individuals who do God's will without ever discovering what they are doing; every person belongs to one

**McCarthyism**

a period of intense suspicion by the American government of American Communists and Communist sympathizers in the early 1950s

**nihilism**

philosophy of nothingness; nothing is or could be important

**oubliette**

a dungeon

**pissant**

a person who is disagreeable simply for the sake of disagreeing; a person who thinks he knows everything and tries to make others feel stupid

**pool–pah**

"shit storm"; the wrath of God

**Puba**

the moon

**reticule**

a woman's bag

**saroon**

to submit to the demands of one's vin–dit

**schnauzer**

breed of dog

**sin–wat**

a man who wants all of somebody's love

**sinookas**

components of an individual's life that can become entangled with those of other members of his karass

**stuppa**

a fogbound child

**vin–dit**

a sudden, very personal shove in the direction of Bokononism

**wampeter**

an object around which the lives of many otherwise unrelated people may revolve; at any time, each karass has two wampeters, one that is becoming more important and one that is becoming less important; the wampeter of Jonah's karass is ice–nine

**wrang–wrang**

a person who steers people away from a line of thinking by reducing that line, with the example of the wrang–wrang's own life, to an absurdity

**zah–mah–ki–bo**

fate; inevitable destiny

# Short Summary

The narrator, Jonah, plans to write a book, The Day the World Ended, describing what important people were doing the day the atomic bomb was dropped on Hiroshima. His research prompts him to contact Newton Hoenikker, the youngest child of Felix Hoenikker, a fictional Nobel laureate physicist who helped develop the weapon. Newt, though only a child on the day the atom bomb was dropped, remembers his father as a brilliant and distant man. Newt also mentions that his brother Frank has been missing for many years, but he provides Jonah with his sister Angela's contact information so that she can share her memories of the day in question. Jonah's attempts to contact Angela go unanswered, but eventually he gets a freelance writing job in Ilium, N.Y., where Felix worked and lived for most of his life.

While in Ilium, Jonah speaks with many of the city's individuals about the infamous Hoenikker family. The children's old colleagues remember them as outcasts and their father as an absent–minded weirdo. Dr. Asa Breed, Felix's former supervisor, and Felix's other colleagues seem to appreciate Felix's contributions to science, but they all tell stories of the ways in which he seemed incomplete or inhuman. He is characterized by his lack of interest in his children and wife, Emily Hoenikker, and many townspeople express dismay at his seeming lack of understanding of basic human emotions and feelings, especially love.

While in Ilium, Dr. Breed tells Jonah about a substance called ice–nine. The substance was a brainchild of Felix Hoenikker, but to Dr. Breed's knowledge he never actually created it. Dr. Breed explains that if a crystal of ice–nine were brought into contact with liquid water, it would change the liquid into a solid form of ice with a very high melting point. Although Jonah does not know it yet, the substance was actually created by Felix Hoenikker and inherited by the Hoenikker children after their father's death.

Shortly after Jonah's visit to Ilium, he receives a writing assignment on the island of San Lorenzo, one of the world's poorest countries. Before he leaves, Jonah learns from a magazine that Frank Hoenikker is also on the island of San Lorenzo working as a member of their government and is expected to be the successor to the island's ailing dictator. It is also through that magazine that Jonah first sees and falls in love with Mona Monzano, the adopted daughter of the island's ruler, "Papa" Monzano. Jonah believes she is the most beautiful woman on earth. On a plane to the island, Jonah finally meets Newton and Angela Hoenikker in person––they are also traveling to the island to celebrate their brother's engagement. Jonah is heartbroken to learn that Frank's engagement is to Mona Monzano. Jonah also begins to learn about Bokononism, a religion that was started by a man named Bokonon to give the people of San Lorenzo hope, despite their pitiful existence.

After a brief and spiritless celebration to commemorate the travelers' arrival, Jonah journeys to his hotel. He is surprised to find he is the first and only guest there (a few of his traveling companions decide to stay at the U.S. Embassy in response to a negative conversation with the hotel's owner). The hotel's owner, Philip Castle, grew up with Mona Monzano and was tutored by Bokonon in his childhood, and he introduces Jonah to some of the basic tenets of Bokononism. Later, Jonah travels to Frank Hoenikker's house, where he speaks with Newton about Dr. Hoenikker and learns that Angela is frustrated by the lack of recognition she believes her father got for his work. She views her father as a saint, and she seems unconcerned with the personal deficiencies that others have described about him.

When Frank arrives home, he convinces Jonah that he would be a better President than Frank, and Frank instructs Jonah that if he became President he would get to marry Mona. After a long discussion, Jonah agrees to become the new President of San Lorenzo. Jonah and Frank decide to announce his succession the next day at the memorial service for the Hundred Martyrs to Democracy.

During the celebration the next day, Papa is very close to death, so Frank and Jonah meet with him. When Papa learns that Jonah will be succeeding him, he makes Jonah promise that he will catch Bokonon. To Papa, science is the only real truth, and the people of the island should only learn scientific truths. Papa calls for his last rites, but when the Catholic priest arrives, Papa turns him away and asks for a Bokononist priest. Jonah leaves to attend the ceremony but is soon called back to Papa's bedside. When he returns, he finds Papa completely frozen with his fingers to his mouth, still poised from swallowing the piece of ice–nine that Frank had given him. Realizing that ice–nine both exists and was used by Frank to obtain power in San Lorenzo, Jonah calls the Hoenikker children to Papa's room. It is revealed that they all have used ice–nine in attempts to find happiness. Moreover, though it was supposed to be a secret, both the U.S. and Russian governments learned of the invention. Angela's husband, a government worker, had married her for possession of ice–nine, and Newt's ex–fiance was actually a Soviet spy who stole part of his piece.

Jonah and the children attempt to clean up Papa's corpse, but there is a disaster at the Hundred Martyrs to Democracy ceremony that causes a plane to crash into Papa's castle, damaging it enough to send his body flying into the ocean. When his body touches the water it instantly turns to ice–nine, causing a chain of ecological disasters. Jonah and Mona escape to a shelter in the remnants of the castle, where they stay for a few days. When they leave the shelter, they discover that the entire ecosystem has been destroyed and tornadoes fill the sky. They search for survivors and discover that almost all of the island's inhabitants traveled to a volcano on the island and committed suicide by swallowing ice–nine. At this sight, Mona laughs and decides to join her people by committing suicide as well.

Newt and a couple of other travelers find Jonah crying beside Mona's corpse a little while later, and they take him back to Frank's house. They have set up a refuge there, where they are able to live as if life as they knew it had not ended. They live there for months, until one day Jonah encounters Bokonon on another part of the island. He is surprised to see the prophet, who informs Jonah that he has written his last addition to the Books of Bokonon. As he reads his final entry aloud, Bokonon closes the novel with a reinforcement of his lack of reverence for life.

Short Summary

# Summary and Analysis of Chapters 1–8

John, the narrator, asks to be called Jonah. He begins the novel with an introduction to the Hoenikker family and the religion of Bokononism. Although Jonah began his life as a Christian, he is now a devoted Bokononist. The Hoenikkers are not Bokononists, but Jonah states that they are members of his "karass." Jonah emphasizes the inability of humans to understand what God is doing and why he is doing it, a fact that is underscored by Jonah's inability to know the true limits of his "karass" group or its total membership. The instrument through which each karass fulfills God's will is called a "kan–kan," and Jonah's planned novel titled The Day the World Ended is the kan–kan through which Jonah was first connected with the Hoenikkers.

Jonah's book is going to chronicle what important Americans did on the day the atomic bomb was dropped on Hiroshima. While he is gathering facts for this work, he runs across a newspaper published by Cornell University's Delta Upsilon fraternity, an organization to which he belonged when he was a student. The publication lists Newt Hoenikker as one of the new pledges for the chapter, and Jonah recognizes him as the son of physicist and Nobel Prize winner Felix Hoenikker. Because Felix Hoenikker was one of the leading scientists behind the development of the atomic bomb, Jonah contacts Newt in an attempt to obtain anecdotes about life in Felix's house the day the bomb was dropped.

Newt's response to Jonah's letter indicates that Newt was only six years old on the day in question. Newt reports that he was playing with toy trucks in his home in Ilium, New York, and his father was in his study fiddling with a loop of string. His father often stayed home from the Research Laboratory of the General Forge and Foundry Company where he worked so he could putter around his Ilium home or his cottage on Cape Cod. Newt notes that his father usually had no fondness for made–up games or tricks because he was more interested in the natural riddles and diversions in the world. Felix hardly ever took interest in books or people, including his own family. Nonetheless, on the day the bomb was dropped, Felix was playing with this string and inadvertently twisted it into a "cat's cradle" configuration. Newt remembers this as the first and only time that his father tried to play with him, and he remembers that Felix left his study and thrust the cat's cradle into his young son's face. Felix attempted to show Newt all of the parts of the cat's cradle, encouraging him to imagine the string as an actual bed for a cat. Newt, however, was distracted by the smell of cigar smoke on his father's clothes and by Felix's frighteningly large pores, ears, and nose. The sight was so startling that Newt burst into tears and ran out of the house. Angela, Newt's sister, was twenty–two years old at the time. She later told Newt that his reaction hurt his father's feelings, but Newt doubts that he hurt his father deeply, since Felix had almost no interest in people. (As a side note, Newt notes a time when he asked his father about Emily Hoenikker, Felix's wife, who had died giving birth to Newt. His father could not remember anything about her.)

When he ran away from his father, Newt found his brother Frank Hoenikker in some bushes outside of their house making bugs fight in a jar. He sat with his brother until Angela came looking for him. When she found him in the bush, Newt was still traumatized and kept repeating how much he hated Felix and how ugly he was. Angela slapped Newt and insisted that their father was one of the greatest men who ever lived. In his letter, Newt attributes Angela's loyalty to the fact that their father was all that she had. Back then she did not have any friends or boyfriends, and her only hobby was playing the clarinet. Angela kept slapping Newt until Frank punched her in the stomach so hard that she fell into the grass crying. She called for their father, but he only stuck his head out of one of the house's windows briefly before returning to his study. People, including his own children, were not Felix's specialty.

Newt finishes his letter with a series of postscripts to clarify its contents. First, he indicates that because of his grades he has flunked out of the medical school at Cornell. Newt also informs Jonah that he is a midget and that his brother Frank is wanted by the Florida police, the FBI, and the Treasury Department for running stolen cars to Cuba. Finally, Newt mentions that he does not want to give the impression that all he does is pity himself, and he expresses his happiness that he is currently engaged to a woman whom he loves. This woman is a Ukrainian midget named Zinka.

Zinka presents herself to the Russian Embassy two weeks after Newt's letter. She wants to return home because she thinks Americans are too materialistic. After Zinka's departure, Newt retreats to his sister's home in Indianapolis.

Analysis

Jonah's preferred name indicates how he thinks of himself in relation to the story he will tell. He says that he chose the name Jonah because he feels as though somebody compels him to be in certain places at certain times. Jonah is also the name of a prophet in the Bible who is compelled to do God's will despite his attempts to disobey. Throughout the novel, Jonah is amazed by the ways in which the seemingly random events in his life seem to be leading him to some inescapable fate. This idea is central to Bokononism, which holds that humans cannot understand God's plan but are unable to resist his will.

The first chapters of the novel introduce the "karass," which is a group called together to do God's will. It is clear from Jonah's writings that the karass is the most important relationship one person can have with another, and he contrasts this kind of relationship with the "granfalloon," a proud but meaningless association of human beings. Newt and Jonah share two granfalloons: their university and their fraternity. Such relationships are comforting, but they also mislead individuals regarding where their loyalties should lie with respect to their destinies and their lives' works.

In Jonah's letter to Newt, he refers to Newt as "Brother," as is the custom of individuals who belong to the same fraternal organization. Newt's reply mentions that he is being kicked out of school and his fraternity because of his grades, so he can no longer call Jonah his brother. Thus Vonnegut comments on the superficial and sometimes nonsensical relationships that individuals force themselves into and which can prevent them from sharing meaningful relationships. In doing so, individuals' granfalloons distract them from the real work of their karasses and ultimately lead people to cause some of the world's more serious problems. Participation in granfalloons can convince a person to fight on behalf of one's family, state, or country, but indirectly; in the grand scheme of things the individual's membership in granfalloons is merely accidental or superficial. Newt's relationship with Jonah is an example of such a superficial relationship, because it is easily ended by Newt's inability to do well in school. When they belonged to the same fraternity, Jonah considered Newt his brother, presumably making them closer than they otherwise would be. This presumption is justified because as soon as Newt is kicked out of school, they no longer have a relationship as brothers, although there was no real change in their relationship as individuals. Superficial social identities have little staying power.

Vonnegut's depiction of Felix Hoenikker is also an introduction to one of the book's overarching themes, the role of deception in making a distinction between right and wrong. Felix, while intelligent enough to be one of the world's greatest scientists, had no concern for or knowledge of the human beings he interacted with every day. He spent very little time with his own children and showed a general indifference to their existence and that of his wife. He viewed his wife, and later his daughter, as caretakers. It is unclear at this point in the novel whether he loved his family or even understood the concept of love, but his failure to show that emotion aids in the portrayal of Felix as the unfeeling scientist who delights in solving tricks and puzzles to the detriment of humanity.

When a scientist commented to Felix that the atomic bomb was the first meeting of science and sin, he responded, "What is sin?" This response shows Felix's relative moral innocence; as a scientist, Felix has never encountered or internalized a concept of morality. Meanwhile, his research had moral implications. The creation of the atomic bomb, while a huge advance for science, was also a moral danger because it dramatically increased the scale of destruction that a nation could inflict on another in a short period of time. Felix's lack of moral responsibility creates a chilling portrayal of scientists who not only express the absentminded qualities of the inventor but who also work with minimal regard for human life. This lack of concern for the plight of others is paralleled, to a lesser extent, in the lives of Newt and Frank. Frank shows no concern for the bugs that he is pitting against each other when Newt finds him outside, and he instead concentrates on his interest in the game of making them fight. Also Newt, in his letter to Jonah, briefly mentions two girls who committed suicide by jumping into a gorge by which he was planning on taking a walk. He seems uninterested in their demise except to relate the surprising fact that they committed suicide because they did not get into the sorority (another granfalloon) they had wanted to enter. There is no sense of sorrow or remorse for these individuals. The unfeeling, unjust lack of concern for other members of humanity will be a repeated theme as Vonnegut's novel progresses.

# Summary and Analysis of Chapters 9–23

Jonah does not follow up with Newt about his family, and his attempts to contact Angela Hoenikker go unanswered. When another journalistic opportunity leads Jonah to Ilium, he attempts to further investigate the Hoenikkers through the contacts they left there. He sets up his first appointment with Dr. Asa Breed, the Vice–President of the research laboratory where Felix had worked. The night before their meeting, Jonah goes to a bar where he meets a prostitute, Sondra, and two bartenders who had known the Hoenikkers. They confide that the whole town thinks of Dr. Hoenikker as an absent–minded professor, while his family is considered a dysfunctional group of losers. The three informants remember Frank Hoenikker as a loser who played with model airplanes and did not involve himself with any people or activities at school. Almost everyone in the town thinks that Dr. Breed is the father of the three Hoenikker children, because it has been rumored that he was in love with Felix's wife, Emily. Dr. Hoenikker was supposed to be the keynote speaker at the trio's graduation from high school, but he did not show up for the ceremony and Dr. Breed had to give a speech instead. He spoke about the virtues of science and argued that if people studied science more, there would not be as much trouble in the world. His words seem to have made an impression on Sandra and the bartender, and they appear excited by a recent report that scientists somewhere have discovered that protein is the secret of life.

The morning after this discussion, Dr. Breed picks up Jonah to escort him to the laboratory where he will conduct the interview about Felix Hoenikker. On the way to the laboratory, Dr. Breed comments on some of the more interesting nuggets of Ilium's history, telling Jonah about a mass murderer who had been hanged in the 16th century near the laboratory's current location. The murderer wrote a song for the occasion. It was primarily about his lack of remorse for the twenty–six people he killed. Dr. Breed, who supervised the creation of the atomic bomb and helped contribute to the deaths of thousands of Japanese citizens, thinks it is outrageous that the murderer had no regrets about directly killing twenty–six people.

Dr. Breed then shifts the subject of conversation to an accident that Emily Hoenikker had while driving a car that her husband had abandoned at an intersection. She was not accustomed to driving the car, and the accident was so serious that it damaged her pelvis. This damage caused her death when she was giving birth to her third child, Newt. Dr. Breed seems emotional when he tells Emily's story, supporting the claim that he might still have feelings for the late Mrs. Hoenikker.

When they arrive at the laboratory, Jonah and Dr. Breed run into a woman named Miss Pefko, who works as a secretary for another scientist at the company. For Jonah's benefit, Dr. Breed tries to get Miss Pefko to talk a little about the research on which her boss is working. Miss Pefko, however, insists that she does not understand anything that the scientist is doing and spends the whole day typing documents that she cannot decipher. She is clearly thrilled to be talking to someone as important as

Dr. Breed, but she disappoints him by emphatically informing him about how little she understands of science and how magical it all seems to her. This characterization peeves Dr. Breed, because he thinks of science as a journey toward truth for humanity, and he wants to eliminate all aspects of superstition and misunderstanding from this venture. He urges Miss Pefko to ask the scientist for whom she works to explain his research to her, but she protests that she is too stupid to understand.

When they arrive at Dr. Breed's office, Jonah meets Dr. Breed's secretary, Miss Faust. She is decorating for the Christmas holiday, and she reminds Dr. Breed that the group of women who type documents for the scientists, the Girl Pool, will be coming later to carol and get their yearly gifts of chocolate bars. Dr. Breed and Jonah go into the inner office, where they begin the interview. The conversation is plagued by the fact that Jonah is hung over and unable to phrase his questions in a way that do not seem contentious to Dr. Breed. After a few questions, Dr. Breed begins to chastise Jonah for not understanding the research being done at the laboratory and thinking that science is just so many attempts to make softer face tissue or better windshield wipers. He argues that true science is an opportunity to increase knowledge, which will lead to increased riches. Although Dr. Breed was Felix's supervisor, he echoes Newt's characterization that Felix Hoenikker basically worked on whatever struck his fancy at the time, with no concern for schedules or reproach. Dr. Breed recalls a time, for example, when the Marines asked Felix to invent a way to eliminate mud. They were tired of wading through mushy terrain, so they asked Felix for a solution that would give them solid ground as they traveled. Although Felix did not appear to give the request much attention, when a Marine general interrupted Felix's lunch to inquire about a possible solution, Felix surmised that it would be possible to rearrange the atoms in water to make it arrange itself as a solid and not a liquid. This arrangement, while not dissimilar from normal ice (which Dr. Breed calls ice–one), would have a very high melting point and be able to turn any liquid to a solid upon contact.

Dr. Breed insists that such a substance does not exist, but Jonah is amazed at the implications of such an invention. It could freeze all of the liquids with which it came into contact, and every liquid with which that liquid came into contact, setting off a chain of events that could freeze all of the world's water sources. Thus, it is an effective and extremely deadly weapon.

Dr. Breed ejects Jonah from his office shortly after this conversation. He does not realize that Felix Hoenikker actually did create ice–nine as his last gift to humanity and, moreover, had told all of his children about his creation on Christmas Eve at their house on Cape Cod. Ice–nine is colored blue–white and has a melting point of 114.4 degrees Fahrenheit. After his death on the night of this revelation, Felix's three children divided the creation among themselves.

Analysis

This section communicates the dangers of technological advancement and laypeople's misunderstanding of science. Vonnegut comically uses Sandra and the bartenders to exemplify this problem as they discuss Dr. Breed's graduation speech and reiterate his view that one day science will solve the world's problems. In a show of misunderstanding, they recall that only two days ago the news had reported that protein had been discovered as the basic secret of life. While protein may have been the most basic component of the report, it is doubtful that such a simple element would have been called the secret to life. But neither Sandra nor the bartender provides an explanation about why protein might be the secret, leading us to believe that they do not actually understand what they are discussing. Their deep faith in something that they ultimately do not understand is important because it relegates science to the level of religion in the minds of many common folk, in that they often see it as fantastic and magical. This misunderstanding is underlined by Dr. Breed's conversation with Miss Pefko. Despite his efforts to assure her of the commonsense aspects of science and the accessibility of scientific research to everyone, it is clear that she does not have the intelligence or motivation to truly understand, as she herself admits. His attempts to laud science as a panacea for ignorance that can be understood by all of humanity are severely contrasted by her response because, for her, science is no different from magic and not worthy of the pedestal where Dr. Breed seems to place it.

Another interesting aspect of Sandra's and the bartenders' conversation with Jonah about protein is that they seem to have derived little real benefit from the discovery. Presumably, scientific research's goal is to improve the wellbeing of humanity, but one of the themes here is research's potential destructiveness over against its contributions to human wellbeing. It may be possible to support scientific research toward concepts that lead to the atomic bomb if there is also a commitment to advancements with healthful instead of lethal effects. But Vonnegut shows through characters like Sandra that most research does little to improve the daily lives of humans. If normal human beings do not benefit in some way from the discovery of the "secret of life," why should they put such stock in science? It is likely that Sandra will spend many more nights in that bar and never see any "real" gains from the protein discovery.

This basic inability for most humans to understand scientific thought and its implications resonates with the lives of the Hoenikker children. All were outcasts from the greater society, and they could find no common ground with their father at home. They were not extraordinary in their desire to be loved and accepted for who they were, but they were uncommon in being so poorly raised by their father that they became social misfits. Their inheritance of ice–nine is dangerous because their conscientious use of the substance relies on their ability to understand both how it works and what larger implications its attributes have for humanity. This understanding is unlikely, though, because beside Dr. Breed and Felix Hoenikker, none of the characters thus far has shown any propensity to understand science.

This section introduces ice–nine, its properties, and its effects. It is important to keep in mind its very high melting point and ability to freeze whatever sources of water it contacts, because these properties will become important later. They help us assess the caution that Felix Hoenikker and his children exhibited in their handling of the substance and help us understand its effects when it finally is used.

# Summary and Analysis of Chapters 24–34

A "wampeter" is an object around which the lives of many otherwise unrelated people may revolve; that is, it is of primary concern to a karass group. Jonah is now convinced that the wampeter of his karass is ice–nine, but immediately following his interview with Dr. Breed he did not know this fact. After leaving Dr. Breed's office, Jonah chats with Miss Faust, who tells him what she knows about Dr. Hoenikker. She seems perplexed by Felix's ability to push aside the sources of normal human pleasure like family and love in exchange for an unobstructed search for truth. Miss Faust explains that no one really knew Felix because his main concern was truth, not people, but she does not believe that truth alone is enough for a person. One time, when Miss Faust said to Felix, "God is love," he replied, "What is God? What is love?" She takes Jonah to Felix's old office, where he marvels at the collection of old broken toys and piles of letters. A plaque on the wall lauds Felix's contributions as invaluable to mankind.

After leaving the laboratory, Jonah visits Felix's tombstone in Ilium. The taxi driver that takes him to the cemetery points out the Hoenikker gravesite, upon which sits a twenty–foot by three–foot monument made of alabaster. Jonah is surprised by the stature of this memorial, and he is even more shocked when he learns that the structure is actually Emily Hoenikker's memorial. Engraved in the memorial are poems from her two oldest children. The poems reveal their devotion to their mother and show their desire for her continued presence in their lives. Curious about what kind of memorial the children have built for their father, one of the greatest American scientists, Jonah treks farther into the cemetery to find a small marble cube that is forty centimeters wide on each side. There is only one word written on it: Father.

After leaving the cemetery, the taxi driver gets the urge to check on his own mother's grave and asks to take a detour to look at it. He then asks to make a short visit to a tombstone salesman across the street from the cemetery. At the shop, Jonah is fascinated by a stone angel that is covered in mistletoe and Christmas decorations. The owner, Marvin Breed, says he is Dr. Asa Breed's brother, and he refuses to sell the angel because it was carved a hundred years earlier by his great–grandfather. Jonah asks Marvin about Felix Hoenikker and the tombstones that the Hoenikker children picked for their parents. Marvin assures him that Felix was not involved in buying Emily's memorial, but that the children got a lot of consolation from the structure and used to visit it many times a year. They bought the monument with the money Felix won for the Nobel Prize. Jonah notes that the namesake of that award is famous for inventing dynamite.

Marvin adds that he was in love with Emily Hoenikker in high school, so much so that he quit playing football in favor of the violin in order to impress her. His older brother Asa then stole her affection on a visit home from college, and Marvin never got over the hurt that he felt from losing Emily. He notes that she was the most beautiful woman he had ever seen, and that she could have had any man she wanted because of her wonderful personality and spirit. When Felix arrived in Ilium, she was smitten with him because she said his mind was tuned to the music of the stars. Marvin sees it as a tragedy that Felix could not appreciate Emily's true beauty, and he shows a great deal of continuing anger toward Dr. Hoenikker.

Marvin acknowledges that Felix was always in a dreamy and gentle state, almost to the point of complete innocence. His seeming disregard for humanity makes Marvin wonder whether Felix was "born dead." Marvin postulates that the reason the world has so many problems is that too many powerful people act like they are dead or have no ties to humanity.

Marvin also expresses concern for Felix's children. He recounts seeing Frank Hoenikker leave in the middle of his father's funeral. He hitchhiked across the street from the cemetery and got into a car with Florida tags, and that was the last anyone ever saw of him. Marvin asserts that Frank's encounter with the police in Florida for running stolen cars to Cuba was a mistake. He believes that Frank accidentally became employed with a model–making shop that was a front for the illegal operation. All he ever wanted to do was make models of cars and battleships. Marvin believes that Frank is dead and that is why no one has heard from him.

Marvin expresses similar concern for Newt Hoenikker, who flunked out of school and was dumped by a Russian midget, and for Angela Hoenikker, whom Felix pulled out of high school her sophomore year to take care of him and the other children. Angela never had any friends, and her only hobby was to play the clarinet. Marvin considers it a miracle that Angela ever found a husband.

During Marvin's and Jonah's conversation, the taxi driver becomes obsessed with the idea of purchasing the stone angel for his mother's tombstone. He offers to buy it from Marvin, but Marvin refuses because of the angel's history. Jonah remarks that it would be impossible to recreate the quality of stone cutting of the angel, but Marvin corrects him, saying that his nephew would be able to do so. His nephew, Dr. Breed's son, worked at the laboratory before the atomic bomb was dropped, but after Hiroshima he quit his job and became a sculptor in Rome.

Marvin tells the story of how the angel was created for a German immigrant whose wife had died of smallpox on their travels west. He ordered the angel for her grave, but then he was robbed of all of his money and could not afford the memorial. He left the state for Indiana and promised to return, but he never did, and the angel stayed in the shop with the immigrant's last name engraved on it. Marvin pulls away the mistletoe on the angel to reveal the man's name. It is the same as Jonah's last name.

Analysis

The exodus of Dr. Breed's son from the world of scientific research to the world of art is another commentary on the destructiveness of technology and its effects on humanity. Vonnegut used Dr. Breed's son as a counterexample to the scientist without a conscience who inflicts his creations on humanity with no concern for their effects. His decision to leave science following the destruction of Hiroshima reveals his discomfort with the implications of his work and again suggests that science is not an absolute good (as Dr. Breed believes). This point is directly tied to Vonnegut's rejection of the truth as innately good, considering his emphasis on the fact that the miraculous discovery of splitting atoms led to destruction and evil results.

Felix's response to Miss Faust's statement that "God is love" supports the characterization of Felix Hoenikker as basically innocent. He presumably has so little interest in the human race that he has not even taken the time to contemplate his own existence on Earth. Without a scientific account of God or love, he has no reason to be concerned about poetic accounts of such things. Further, his question about the definition of love reveals his indifference to human feeling. If he does not know what love is, he probably has never experienced the emotion and does not feel the same ties to other humans that most people feel. This deficiency makes him unable to take into consideration the moral implications of his work. He cannot understand basic concerns about survival or personal wellbeing, so his work is ultimately amoral. If science is amoral, the search for truth is not simply good; one must seek truth for the right reasons and then use knowledge wisely and morally.

When Miss Faust makes her comment about God, she is responding to Felix's request that she tell him an absolute truth. Miss Faust offers a religious kind of truth, but Felix asks for a scientific kind. This miscommunication highlights the dichotomy between science and religion, because at their most basic levels, they are operating in two separate dimensions, the natural and the divine. Miss Faust sees God as a real being who exists, but if God is ineffable, science can find nothing testable about God in nature. The quest for truth must confront this tension, and many people choose science or religion without making sense of the tension. Miss Faust's belief that scientific truth is not enough to sustain a person, however, is a separate issue that Vonnegut addresses later. Although truth seemed to be enough for Felix, he is presented as almost inhuman and, therefore, unrepresentative of humanity.

Jonah finds intriguing the different ways in which the Hoenikker parents were memorialized in light of their respective contributions to humanity. The Hoenikker children used their father's Nobel Peace Prize money to create a gigantic tombstone for their mother, representative of the extremely large role she played in their lives. On it they wrote poems about their relationship with her, and Marvin comments that they visited the monument often. Felix, in contrast, requested to be memorialized with a relatively small cube that simply reads "Father." This may seem disproportionate, since Felix is presumably one of the more important figures of the 20th century, but the idea of creating a huge memorial to someone who did not understand or care about other human beings would be even more out of joint.

Though Felix wanted a small memorial and his children were not given a choice in the matter, it is unclear whether his children would have done more for him were they given the chance. They chose to memorialize their parents on the basis of their parenting rather than their world significance. Angela seems to be the only person who really appreciates her father as he was, and she appears to be the only Hoenikker child with any motivation to build him a shrine. Frank Hoenikker did not even stay for his father's entire memorial service. Instead, he left Ilium never to be seen again.

Marvin's portrayal of the Hoenikker children is one of great pity and sympathy. As a man who has worked at the intersection between the living and the dead, he seems to have the most insight about the struggles the Hoenikkers faced with their father. Marvin did not see Felix Hoenikker as innocent, because he brought great pain to the world and his family. He always got everything he wanted, and he selfishly used his daughter to continue his childlike existence following his wife's death. As long as he was comfortable and had some idea or toy to amuse him, Felix could not care less about anyone else in the world.

The stone angel is another example of how God's will brings individuals to a certain place at a certain time, much as had happened to Jonah. The series of fateful events leading to Jonah's discovery of his last name on the angel seem to be perfectly orchestrated, reaffirming his idea that whatever will be, will be.

# Summary and Analysis of Chapters 35–43

On the way back to his hotel, Jonah stops by the hobby shop where Frank Hoenikker used to work. He meets the owner, Jack, who takes Jonah to the basement to see one of Frank's creations. It is an expansive, intricate model city. Jack describes with pride how dedicated Frank has been to the project and points out the amazing insight Frank has shown as a city planner. Jack mentions that his wife left him a week ago, but he shows no emotion when relaying this information. When talking about Frank Hoenikker, however, and the tragedy of his premature death, Jack becomes quite emotional because of what the world lost in his passing.

After returning home from his travels in Ilium, Jonah finds his apartment completely wrecked by Sherman Krebbs, the artist he allowed to stay in his home while he traveled. Jonah met Sherman at a cocktail party where Sherman presented himself as the National Chairman of Poets and Painters for Immediate Nuclear War. While Jonah was gone, Sherman made three hundred dollars' worth of phone calls, set a couch on fire, killed Jonah's cat, and broke appliances in his apartment. Sherman also wrote a poem on the refrigerator in excrement and left a note around the dead cat's neck that said "Meow." In retrospect, Jonah considers Krebbs a "wrang–wrang" in his karass, a person who steers people away from a line of thought by the example of the wrang–wrang's own life. Krebbs's horrific treatment of Jonah's apartment and cat serve to deter Jonah from a nihilistic philosophy, allowing him to stay receptive to the teachings of Bokonon that he will be exposed to in the future.

One Sunday after his return from Ilium, Jonah discovers where Frank Hoenikker is residing from a supplement to the *New York Sunday Times*. The supplement describes the island of San Lorenzo, and Jonah is drawn to it because on its cover is the most beautiful woman he has ever seen, Mona Monzano. Inside the publication are pictures of the island and facts about its economy and people, but more importantly there are pictures of Frank Hoenikker standing with the island's dictator, "Papa" Monzano. The supplement identifies Frank as "the blood son of Dr. Felix Hoenikker" several times, and it notes that he is now serving as the Minister of Science and Progress for the island. There is an article describing how Frank happened upon San Lorenzo after being stranded at sea in the Caribbean. When he reached the island, he thought it was a mirage like Fata Morgana, but quickly realized the island was real and that he was being put into jail because he did not have a passport. But he was quickly rescued by "Papa" Monzano after the dictator found out about his ties to Felix Hoenikker, and Frank has since served as an advisor to the leader.

After learning of Frank's fate, Jonah is given a reporting assignment about a sugar millionaire, Julian Castle, who has spent the last twenty years in San Lorenzo working in a hospital he built for the people there. Prior to his arrival on San

Lorenzo, Castle was known for his debauchery, but now he is a respected doctor. His only son, Philip Castle, is the manager and owner of the Casa Mona hotel at which Jonah will be staying during his visit.

On the airplane to San Lorenzo, Jonah sits beside a couple, Horlick and Claire Minton. Horlick has just been appointed American Ambassador to San Lorenzo, after serving as a diplomat in numerous other countries around the world. Horlick and Claire are a perfect "duprass," which is a karass composed of only two people. Jonah tries to make conversation with the Mintons, but he never seems to say the right thing and they do not seem interested in including him in their intimate chats.

Later on the plane, Jonah wanders back to a bar area where he meets H. Lowe Crosby, a bicycle maker who is traveling to San Lorenzo to start up a bicycle factory. His wife Hazel is a Hoosier, and she is excited to learn that Jonah is also from Indiana. Hazel delights in the many successful Hoosiers of the world because they are all members of her granfalloon, and she asks Jonah to call her "Mom" because of the bond they apparently share simply on the basis of their common birthplace. Crosby and Jonah begin discussing the culture of San Lorenzo, and Crosby tells him about the large amount of discipline the people there have because of the strict laws. He describes the hook, a method of execution that requires that the offender be placed sideways on a metal hook and hung from it as an example to the rest of the population. The Crosbys have seen a replica of the hook at the waxworks in London, and it looked so real that Hazel wanted to vomit.

Analysis

Jack shows a great deal of pride in the accomplishments of Frank Hoenikker, considering him as something of a national treasure. Frank's devotion to his model–making is enviable to Jack, and he deeply regrets that Frank died so young. Jack's belief in the great impact that Frank's model–making could have had on the world is a parody intended to reveal the futility of human ventures. Whether Frank had been making toy cars or painting the Sistine Chapel, nothing that he created would be important in the multi–million year history of the world. Jack's concern for the world's loss, in contrast with his lack of concern for his loss of his wife, shows how confused humans' priorities can become with respect to the importance of their creations.

Frank's apparent contribution to humanity (his model town) is not unlike the contributions of Felix Hoenikker. It appears that Frank devoted his life to creating a world that he could perfect and control, and he did so to the detriment of personal relationships. That Frank is actually engaged to Mona (as Jonah discovers later) may seem to contradict this characterization, but remember that Felix Hoenikker also had a wife and three children. It is also interesting to contrast the personalities of Newt and Angela in this context. Angela herself appears to have had difficulty relating to others; many of the townspeople remember her having no friends or boyfriends. Newt, for his part, seems relatively well adjusted as compared with his siblings and father. He was a member of a fraternity, and he seems to Jonah to have tremendous dignity and patience. It is likely that Vonnegut made Newt a midget as a small commentary on what virtue and success can look like. This is not to say that Newt is perfect, but it is noteworthy that the most obviously abnormal character seems to have the most common sense and social capital thus far.

H. Lowe and Hazel Crosby represent ignorant, greedy Americans. They are oblivious to the feelings of those around them, but they constantly seek validation in the form of glorifying granfalloons and seeking others' agreement with their opinions. The Crosbys represent the dangers of dogmatic religious and national identity. The most important aspect of the islanders to Hazel is that they are Christian and speak English, while H. Lowe repeatedly offers his agreement with the San Lorenzans' policy of punishing even the most negligible offenses with the hook. Both characters show a lack of understanding and appreciation for the cultural differences between themselves and the San Lorenzans, while attempting to ignore the idea that people who are not like them are not necessarily bad or backwards. Hazel's delight in finding out that Jonah is a Hoosier only speaks to this attempt to categorize people through her own perspective alone. The Crosbys are friendly with Jonah because he is one of them.

Jonah's irrational trust in Krebbs and Krebbs' subsequent mistreatment of that trust show how ignorant humans can be of their own fates. It is meant to be clear to the reader that lending one's apartment to a complete stranger is not a good idea, but Jonah shows a complete lack of insight in this regard. This scenario is helpful in supporting the Bokononist theme that humans cannot understand God's will, but it also reinforces the theme of the general idiocy of man.

When Jonah falls in love with Mona the moment he sees her, the love at first sight is probably just lust. He has no foundation for his love other than her appearance, but he is at once convinced that having her would make him happy. Thus, he is more than willing to travel to the island of San Lorenzo. As the story will show, however, this is just another fruitless human pursuit that will be played out according to God's will, whether it is beneficial to Jonah or not.

# Summary and Analysis of Chapters 44–55

When Jonah returns to his seat, Horlick Minton mentions that he overheard the Crosbys telling Jonah that the Mintons are Communist sympathizers. Horlick attempts to clarify that he is not a Communist, just a pessimist about the world's sympathies regarding the United States. He and Claire assert that Americans cannot expect to be loved throughout the world at all times because it is in human nature to hate other people. And since Americans are people like the rest, they should expect to be hated at times, too. Because the nation is in the midst of McCarthyism at this point, Horlick has lost his job because of his wife's statement to newspapers regarding America's less than perfect status on the world scene.

After this discussion, the Mintons begin explaining that Frank Hoenikker is no longer on the run from the U.S. government because he has relinquished his citizenship by joining San Lorenzo's government. They allow Jonah to examine a manuscript about San Lorenzo that was written by Philip Castle, and Jonah gets his first exposure to the teachings of Bokonon.

Philip Castle's book describes Bokononism as arising from the theory of "Dynamic Tension." Bokonon believes that the only way to create a good society is to maintain a high tension between good and evil. Bokonon, who was born on the island of Tobago in 1891, was originally named Lionel Boyd Johnson and was known for his wild and fun–loving behavior. When he turned twenty, he sailed in a ship called *Lady's Slipper* to London, where he attended the London School of Economics and Politics. He fought in the First World War. After traveling to many parts of the world, he and a man named Earl McCabe encountered a violent sea storm and were washed up onto the shore of San Lorenzo completely naked. Bokonon marveled at the experience of entering a new world naked, and he likened it to being "born again" in the Christian sense. The natives of the island could not say his given name, Lionel Boyd Johnson, so he adopted their pronunciation: "Bokonon." Shortly after he arrived on the island, Bokonon's shattered ship was found on shore. It was later painted and made the bed of the island's chief executive, and Bokonon crafted a legend that when the end of the world was near, that boat would sail again.

Before Jonah is able to read more about Bokonon, Hazel insists that he meet the other two Hoosiers on the plane, Newt and Angela Hoenikker. Jonah greets the two Hoenikkers, and Angela apologizes for never responding to Jonah's requests for stories about her father. She is surprised that Newt wrote a letter about the day the atomic bomb was dropped, and she expresses concern that his memories of the events are inaccurate. Angela treats Newt as a child, and Jonah is impressed by how calm and accepting Newt is in response to her insensitive comments about his inability to function like any other adult. Angela expresses the view that Dr. Hoenikker was a saint among men and, while showing Jonah pictures of her loved ones, she points out both her strikingly handsome husband and Frank's future fiancée, Mona Monzano. Jonah is shocked by both of these discoveries, and he continues to feel unsettled while he listens to Angela's story about how her husband Harrison Conners contacted her in the weeks after her father's death. They were married only two weeks after that first meeting.

When Jonah returns to his seat, he searches the index of Philip Castle's manuscript for information about Mona Monzano and tries to ignore the pain he feels from knowing she is going to be engaged to Frank Hoenikker. He shows her section of the index to the Mintons, and he learns that Claire worked for many years as an indexer. She asserts that no author should ever index his own novel, but because Castle did so, she can tell a lot of things about his personality. She reveals that Castle is an insecure man who is in love with Mona but will never marry her because he is a homosexual.

Analysis

Vonnegut uses the Horlicks to comment on the dangers of xenophobia and blind patriotism following the Second World War. Due to extensive propaganda about the United States' enemies during the war, Americans retained a great amount of fear and misunderstanding of the nations surrounding them when the conflict ended. This fear allowed for the intensification of the Cold War and the race for nuclear arms, but it also created a lack of tolerance for "anti–American" or pro–Communist sentiments. The Horlicks' statements about Americans and their unwillingness to think of themselves as similar to other nations' inhabitants (that is, liked by some, disliked by others), are misconstrued as pro–Communist sentiments because it was so rare at that time for anyone to speak negatively about America, no matter how true that negativity may have been.

This is an interesting paradox, because America's wars in the name of freedom inspire the desire to suppress any question of American policies or America's standing in the world. Vonnegut highlights this paradox when the Crosbys distrust the Horlicks. The insular single–mindedness that the Crosbys portray shows the danger and ridiculousness of xenophobia. In fact, by portraying the Crosbys as "typical Americans," Vonnegut provides support for Claire's guess that Americans could be disliked by their neighbors.

It is rather humorous when Claire reveals that she can tell certain things about Philip Castle through an analysis of his index. She states that Castle is insecure——but Jonah is quick to remind her that most people are insecure. Her other declarations about his sexual preference and love for Mona are not easily verifiable, and it is unclear how she is interpreting the evidence to reach these conclusions. It is impossible, therefore, to tell whether she can actually interpret indexes correctly, and this may be another example of an unimportant and fruitless human pursuit. Even so, the episode points out that readers might be able to learn a great deal by considering the choices made by an author, even at the level of an index.

Claire's characterization of Philip's relationship with Mona contrasts with Jonah's feelings for Mona. Jonah has based all of his desire for her on her appearance and is likely sexually attracted to her—can he possibly love her at this point? According to Claire, Philip is in love with Mona but is a homosexual, meaning that he is not sexually attracted to her. It may seem strange to think about a person being in love with someone to whom he is not sexually attracted, but using Jonah as a reversal of that situation makes it more plausible. Angela's portrayal of her father shows a complete lack of concern for his inventions' negative effects on humanity and his poor treatment of her and her family. She guards his reputation like that of a saint and cannot accept the truth of his negligence. Yet, she acquired some of his negligent behavior, which allowed her to marry Harrison Conners in exchange for ice–nine. A shipwreck or a plane crash could have released the ice–nine they were carrying to San Lorenzo into the ocean, creating a global disaster. The Hoenikkers, however, could not see past their own selfishness.

# Summary and Analysis of Chapters 56–66

As Jonah reads Philip Castle's manuscript, he learns more about the island of San Lorenzo and its history. When Bokonon landed on the island of San Lorenzo, the people were in a state of poverty and illness. All of the land was owned by either Castle Sugar, a company founded by Julian Castle's grandfather, or the Catholic Church. The island had switched ownership many times since its first discovery, and no one seemed to mind when a new controlling power came to claim San Lorenzo because there were no valuable resources on the island. The only person who believed the island was valuable prior to Bokonon's arrival was a crazy man named Tum–wumba. He was a dictator who had large fortifications built on one side of the island to protect it from attack, although no one ever had a reason to attack it. Fourteen hundred San Lorenzans died while building the fortifications, and about half of that group were executed for substandard zeal. Thus, when McCabe and Bokonon landed on the island, their plan to make the island into a Utopia set them apart from all of its previous owners, who had only sought control of it to exploit nonexistent natural resources.

Jonah is engrossed in Castle's book when Newt taps him on the shoulder and asks if he will join Newt at the plane's bar for a drink. Jonah accepts, and soon Newt is speaking frankly with Jonah about his relationship with Zinka and saying that he does not regret the moments they spent together at their love nest at his father's house on Cape Cod. Soon H. Lowe Crosby joins them at the bar, and he begins to complain about pissants, people who are disagreeable simply for the sake of disagreeing or who go out of their way to make others feel stupid. H. Lowe says a couple of insensitive things about Newt's stature, but Newt shows no concern about his comments. The three discover that they all attended Cornell, and they delight in that granfalloon for a moment before H. Lowe Crosby asks Newt why he recognizes Newt's name. As he tries to recall something about a Russian midget dancer, Newt tactfully steers Crosby's memory, and they return to their seats for landing.

When they land in San Lorenzo, Jonah is struck by the island's destitute state. Bokonon, McCabe, and "Papa" Monzano's attempts to raise the island and its people from their squalor are in vain, as all attempts will be because the island is eternally unproductive. While exchanging their dollars for the island's currency, Corporals, the travelers notice signs hung all over the buildings. The signs warn against the practice of Bokononism. There are also reward posters for Bokonon's capture and further warnings against "foot play." Everyone is confused about these signs, but they cannot spend much time on the issue because they are greeted by a huge crowd of San Lorenzans once they leave customs. The people are all very pale and thin, and no one looks healthy. Although there are babies in the crowd, none of them is crying, and although there are dogs in the streets, none barks, so the only sounds that can be heard are occasional coughs from the townspeople. "Papa" Monzano, Mona, and Frank Hoenikker show up in a black limousine, and after the crowd sings the national anthem and Mona plays the xylophone, Papa comes to greet the travelers.

Papa speaks English fairly well as he welcomes the travelers to his island, mistaking Crosby for Horlick Minton. After being corrected, Papa begins his welcome again, but he is struck by an intense internal pain that leaves him teary-eyed. He recovers and allows Horlick Minton to make a speech in which he expresses gratitude for the villagers' hospitality. Horlick pledges that every American schoolchild will know of the sacrifice of San Lorenzo's Hundred Martyrs to Democracy. Although Jonah does not know who the martyrs are at the time, he later learns from the island's only cab driver that the Hundred Martyrs were a group of volunteers who were to be sent to the United States to aid in the war effort after the bombing of Pearl Harbor. They had barely left the harbor of Bolivar, San Lorenzo's capital and only city, when their ship was sunk by a German submarine and they all died.

Following Horlick's speech, Papa invites all of the travelers to Frank and Mona's engagement party the next day at his palace. He is mid-sentence when he suddenly doubles over in pain, commands the crowd to disperse, and then collapses in front of the microphone. He is not dead, but he struggles to speak as he tells Frank that Frank should succeed him as President because Frank has the power of science. Papa asserts that science is the strongest thing there is, and before passing out he utters the words "science" and "ice."

At this point, Jonah glances at Mona and notices that she is standing very close to one of the pilots at the ceremony with a very calm look. The pilot has a strange look frozen on his face, and when Jonah looks down he notices that Mona has removed her sandal and is using her foot to massage the instep of the pilot's foot.

Analysis

The story of San Lorenzo's history and Tum-wumba is another reminder of Vonnegut's theme that all human pursuits are fruitless. Throughout the centuries, control of the island has transferred hands as different countries have tried to assert their power by capturing it from other countries. But after doing so, each country realizes that the island has no strategic value or resources. This situation creates a pointless game in which a nation takes control, loses it, forgets about it, and fights for control again years later. This is a parody of humans' desire for control for the mere sake of control. Tum-wumba, by contrast, is one of the only people who ever saw the island as valuable, although the reason he believed it to be so is unclear, save his insanity.

Half of those who died building Tum-wumba's fortifications were executed for not being sufficiently excited. It is easy to see how substandard excitement may have been a problem for the islanders, given their lot in life. The travelers' reception at the celebration is a good example of the islanders' lifelessness. It is comical to think of this reception as a celebration, because none of the islanders look or act as if they care about the newcomers except as curiosities. But their behavior makes sense because Jonah and the other visitors seem unlikely to have any real affect on their lives. Their days will still be filled with hard labor and starvation, as were the days of their ancestors.

The government of San Lorenzo exploits the people to gain some advantage over them. The island's leaders live in comfortable settings and relative wealth, while the San Lorenzans literally have nothing to call their own. When Bokonon attempted to spread the island's wealth more equally, he realized that there were just enough resources to leave every person unhappy with what he had gotten. This is the first setting in which Bokonon is presented as an antagonist to all of the other characters, and the visitors are intrigued by the wanted posters and warnings against following his teachings.

"Papa" Monzano asserts his desire for Frank to succeed him, and by doing so he perpetuates the myth that science has done good for the San Lorenzans. There is no indication that Frank's job as a scientist will make him a successful leader. Further, there are no successful leaders, because as Bokonon teaches and as the island's experience attests, all human pursuits are useless. Vonnegut leads us to wonder how much better off we are than these people after all.

Newt tells Jonah that he does not regret his relationship with Zinka. It has already been revealed that this relationship resulted in the Russians obtaining ice-nine, but Newt shows no remorse for the danger he has exposed the world to with his recklessness. Again, his attitude supports Vonnegut's theme that people do not understand science well enough to make intelligent decisions about its use—technology in the hands of people with no conscience endangers all of humanity. To Newt, his relationship with Zinka is worth the destruction of the world, even though it is clear that she does not and never did love him.

# Summary and Analysis of Chapters 67–76

Papa does not die that day. The travelers are all taken to their respective lodgings for the evening. The Crosbys and Jonah are taken to the Casa Mona hotel, and on the way they learn more about San Lorenzo and Bokonon from the cab driver. The driver says Bokonon is a very bad man whom no San Lorenzan is stupid enough to follow because that person would be punished with the hook if captured. Jonah discovers that he understands the San Lorenzan dialect very well, so he translates for the Crosbys. When they arrive at the hotel, they find that they are the first and only guests. Crosby does not want to be the first person to sign the register, so he wanders off to talk to a man who is creating a mosaic of Mona Monzano's face. He returns shortly and declares that he wants the man fired because he is a puissant. A clerk informs Crosby that the man, Philip Castle, owns the hotel. The Crosbys leave the hotel and demand to be housed with the Mintons at the American embassy instead. Jonah has a conversation with Philip that reveals Philip to be very sarcastic and smart. Philip grew up with Mona Monzano and is a devout Bokononist. Because he is American, he does not have to fear punishment for his religion, and he reveals that Bokonon was his and Mona's tutor when they were growing up.

Jonah is shown to his room, which he discovers does not have sheets on the bed or toilet paper in the bathroom. The hotel is built with walls of stone on three of its sides and a wall of glass on the fourth side, so tourists can view the harbor and the airport without having to see the dilapidation of the rest of San Lorenzo. As Jonah travels the hallways looking for a maid to give him toilet paper, he accidentally walks in on a couple of painters lying on a bookshelf in one of the hotel's rooms. Each is on his back with his ankles in his hands and eyes closed, and they are pressing the soles of their bare feet together. Jonah interrupts them, and they fall to the ground in fear and beg that he not tell anyone what he has seen. They are afraid of being put on the hook, since they were engaging in the Bokononist ritual of boko–maru. Bokononists believe it is impossible to be sole to sole with a person without loving that person, so the practice is like a mingling of awareness.

Jonah returns to his room to find Philip Castle putting rolls of toilet paper in the bathroom. They begin to discuss why Philip built a hotel instead of following in his father's footsteps at the hospital, and he tells Jonah about a time that a ship transporting wicker furniture was wrecked on the island. The only survivors of the wreck were the furniture and some rats, so some people on the island got new furniture and others got the bubonic plague. Over a thousand San Lorenzans died from the plague, and his father could do nothing to stop the epidemic. One night, Philip stayed up with his father at the hospital to look for patients who were still alive and could be treated. After going from bed to bed and finding only dead bodies, his father began giggling uncontrollably as he put his hand on his son's head. His father turned to Philip and told him, "Someday this will all be yours."

During Jonah's conversation with Philip, Frank calls to request Jonah's presence at his house that evening. Jonah leaves the hotel for Frank's house on Mount McCabe, and when he arrives he meets the only plump San Lorenzan, Frank's servant Stanley. After being shown the room in which he will sleep for the night, Jonah goes to Frank's balcony to admire the waterfall around which the building is built. Newt is sleeping out there, and Jonah surveys one of his paintings, which appears to be a series of black scratches on the canvas. When Newt is stirred by a noise in the distance, they begin discussing the painting, which Newt says is a depiction of a "cat's cradle." He expresses dismay at the fact that millions of parents teach their children that a twisted string is supposed to represent a cat in a cradle and then wonder why their children grow up crazy. Newt believes the parents must be the crazy ones, because it is obvious that there is "no damn cat, and no damn cradle."

A little later, the rest of the Hoenikkers and Julian Castle join Jonah and Newt on the balcony. Julian Castle appears rather disagreeable and does not like the idea of assigning meanings to things experienced or created by humans. He at first likens Newt's painting to a rendering of hell, but after learning that it is a cat's cradle, he is impressed at the idea that the painting is about meaninglessness. He asserts that "man is vile, and man makes nothing worth making, knows nothing worth knowing." With this statement, Castle flings the painting out into the waterfall.

Analysis

Philip Castle's story about his night at the hospital with his father reveals the state of humanity in its efforts to save itself. Julian Castle was fighting a lost battle by trying to save the sufferers of the bubonic plague, and he appreciated the irony of his efforts to ignore the hopelessness of the situation. When he could not deny the ridiculous situation of being a doctor with no way to cure, he could not help but laugh. Further, he realized that his frustration would only be passed on to his son. This transfer expresses the futility of preparing future generations to bring happiness and peace to mankind.

It therefore becomes more apparent why Philip Castle has taken up a more relaxed lifestyle of painting and running a hotel. Although both Philip and Julian are Bokononists who believe firmly in the fruitlessness of human pursuits, they dedicate their time to ambitious activities such as running a hospital and writing a book. Knowing the hopelessness of life could have made it easy for them to choose to give up and spend the rest of their lives basking in the sun or making random choices, but they instead seem relatively driven and even somewhat successful. Perhaps, knowing that their failure to make a difference in the world is due to their being human rather than their particular inadequacies makes it easier for them to work without worrying about the outcome. Since they have nothing to lose, they can spend time doing the things that they find fulfilling in the moment, even if it all turns out to be worthless in the end. Thus, Philip Castle's empty hotel is not strictly a failure; it is a manifestation of his ability to pursue whatever dreams he wants, without concern for success or for anyone else's happiness.

Newt's painting and his constant reference to the cat and the cradle deepen the symbolism of the title of the novel. Cat's cradle is the game that Felix chose to play as the atomic bomb destroyed part of the world, and it is a perfect example of the meaninglessness of all human pursuits. There is no cat or cradle in the strings that comprise the game, yet millions of children are encouraged to imagine them for entertainment alone. There is no truth in the game, where the referent "cat's cradle" does not appropriately refer to a cat or a cradle. The oddly shaped string hardly even represents a cat's cradle. Thus, the object is an exemplar of the novel's suggestions about life and humanity insofar as it represents life as an assortment of lies and misunderstandings that hardly make sense of the chaos.

Despite Newt's apparent agreement during Julian Castle's rant about the pointlessness of life, he undoubtedly is surprised when Castle tosses his work into the waterfall. To be consistent with his worldview, he should be completely uninterested in whether the painting survives or not, but his surprise at Castle's reaction reveals that he probably valued that painting as more than an immediate source of pleasure. It is easy for Newt to agree with the tenets of Bokononism in theory, but it is much more difficult for him to apply them to his own life, because there remain things that genuinely matter to him.

Jonah's first exposure to the ritual of boko–maru occurs when he catches workers performing it at the hotel. He has little understanding or concern for what they are doing. It is both comical and creative that Vonnegut chose "the mingling of awareness" through touching feet to be one of the most important rituals in Bokononism, and it likely speaks to the novel's presentation of the pointlessness and ridiculousness of religious rituals in general. Feet are not particularly revered in American culture, and they seem an unlikely route to the soul. Yet, there is a real intimacy in the act of touching feet. After all, human contact must begin somewhere.

# Summary and Analysis of Chapters 77–83

Remembering that Julian Castle is the primary physician at the House of Hope and Mercy in the Jungle, Jonah inquires about the health of Papa. Julian replies that Papa hates him, because at the hospital it is customary to administer the last rites of the Bokononist church to those who want them. He shocks Jonah by informing him that everybody on San Lorenzo is a devout Bokononist, per Bokonon and Earl McCabe's agreement when they landed on the island. Castle notes that the religion of Bokononism is the only source of hope for the residents of San Lorenzo, and that all of the people accept Bokonon's lies. He assures Jonah that he too will one day be a Bokononist.

When they rejoin the Hoenikkers on the terrace, everyone has cocktails except Julian, who lost a kidney from his days as a playboy. Both Newt and Angela become very drunk, and Angela starts complaining about how underappreciated her father is and what a disgrace it is that so many people were paid more than he was. She is on the verge of tears when Newt suggests that she play her clarinet for Jonah and Julian to make her feel better. After Angela leaves to get her clarinet, Newt admits that she has been having a tough time because her husband is mistreating her and cheating with other women. When Jonah expresses his misunderstanding—he thought Angela's marriage was happy—Newt holds up his fingers and asks, "See the cat? See the cradle?"

When Angela returns, she begins to play her clarinet, and Jonah is shocked by the beauty and virtuosity of her music. He is so flabbergasted that such an unattractive woman can produce such a beautiful sound that he makes a comment to Julian Castle about the incomprehensibility of life. Castle discourages him from trying to understand life and tells him to simply pretend to understand it, as Bokonon teaches one should. Jonah then asks Castle for a copy of the Books of Bokonon. Castle replies that copies are hard to come by and incomplete because Bokonon adds to them every day. Newt scoffs at Jonah's interest, stating, "Religion… See the cat? See the cradle?"

Frank does not appear for dinner but phones Jonah to make sure that he will stay on the mountain that night. When Jonah asks why Frank needs to see him, Frank replies with the phrase "zah–mah–ki–bo," which Julian explains means fate or inevitable destiny. Julian then begins to explain that Papa Monzano is dying of cancer and that his physician is Dr. Schlichter von Koenigswald, who served as a camp physician at Auschwitz for six years. He now works at the House of Hope and Mercy. Castle estimates that at Koenigswald's current rate of healing, the number of people whose lives he has saved will equal the number of people he let die by the year 3010.

Analysis

After they realized that a Utopia would be impossible, Bokonon and McCabe devised a religion as an instrument of hope for the people in response to the ineffectiveness of any governmental or economic reform. Bokonon saw truth as the enemy of the people, so he made it his life's mission to create better and better lies in order to give the people of San Lorenzo hope. One of the most important lies was that McCabe would take on the role of dictator to the people and condemn the religion of Bokononism, on the premise that conflict and oppression gives the religious life of the people more zest. Thus the conflict between science and religion, to the extent that it is represented by the conflict betwen the dictator and the prophet, is manufactured rather than real.

It is significant, moreover, that this lie ultimately had to confront reality. The people of San Lorenzo found themselves actors in a wonderful morality play that they could understand and from which they could derive hope, but this play seemed to require that the prophet be all good and the dictator to be all evil. Julian Castle believes the strain of these roles caused both men to go crazy. McCabe never made any real efforts to catch Bokonon, because it would have rendered his own position irrelevant. Papa Monzano also realized this truth, so his attempts to catch Bokonon were also somewhat half–hearted. The rulers cannot participate fully in the lies; they must respect reality in order to achieve their goals.

Angela's concern about her father's salary while in the midst of San Lorenzo's poverty shows her characteristic lack of concern for the suffering of humanity. She does not take into account that most San Lorenzans would have considered his salary a fortune, nor is she placated by the fact that his salary and prize money allowed him to afford a vacation house on Cape Cod and a twenty–foot memorial for Emily Hoenikker.

Vonnegut presents Dr. Koenigswald as another example of the pointlessness of human pursuits. He was responsible for the deaths of millions of innocent people in Germany, but now he has traveled to San Lorenzo with the intent of saving San Lorenzans' lives. It is unclear whether he believes that his work will release him of the guilt that he bears from his work with the Nazis, but Vonnegut creates the possibility that such work can serve as repentant penance. Likewise, Julian Castle has chosen to dedicate his life to the people of San Lorenzo and his hospital, despite his past as a playboy and womanizer. He, too, has much for which to repent, and perhaps San Lorenzo provides his opportunity to do so. But the novel challenges the idea that their work on the island will help erase the evil that they performed earlier in their lives. Moreover, there is something unjust about thinking that for Koenigswald to repent, he must create a 1:1 ratio of people he killed to people he later saves.

# Summary and Analysis of Chapters 84–93

Frank has not returned home by the time Julian Castle is leaving, so Jonah finds himself on the terrace with Angela and Newt. They are admiring the few bright lights in the city when they notice a convoy heading toward the mountain. Soon the house is surrounded by soldiers, who say they were ordered to protect the house and the new president. Despite Jonah's protests that the new president is not in the house, the soldiers stay to keep watch.

Shortly after, there is a power outage in all of San Lorenzo. These are common, so the guests are given gas lanterns and resume their conversation. Jonah is still rattled from his conversation with Frank. He cannot stop himself from thinking about the stone angel back in Ilium. Angela and Newt are discussing their father's twin brother, who was a music box manufacturer, and his sister, who raised schnauzers. Angela comments about how different family members can become, and Jonah agrees before leaving the terrace to find a copy of the Books of Bokonon.

He asks Stanley for a copy. Stanley grumbles that the texts are filth and that anyone who reads them should be placed on the hook, but he produces a copy for Jonah from Frank's bedside table. Jonah begins to search for an explanation of zah–mak–ki–bo, but the text is too thick. He settles for reading about Bokonon's cosmogony instead. According to the Books of Bokonon, Borasisi held Pabu in his arms and hoped that she would bear him a fiery child. When Pabu gave birth to children that were cold and did not burn, Borasisi threw them away in disgust, and these became the planets. Then Pabu was cast away, and she went to live with her favorite child, Earth, because the people on Earth looked up to her and loved her. Bokonon writes of this cosmogony, a theory of his own creation, that it, like everything else, is nothing more than foma.

The next thing Jonah remembers is waking up to a series of bangs and flashes of light. He is so startled that he believes he is going to die, until he runs into Angela and Newt fleeing from their beds. They laugh at being so startled, and they note that Jonah has somehow grabbed his wallet and passport, while the Hoenikkers are both grasping medium–sized thermoses. Jonah does not know at the time that these thermoses contain ice–nine, which the Hoenikkers carried with them on the plane to San Lorenzo. The source of the banging actually is Frank Hoenikker attempting to fix the generators at the house, and Newt and Angela manage to hide their thermoses by the time Frank makes it inside the house with his future bride, Mona.

Frank immediately takes Jonah aside and asks to speak with him in private, so the two go to Frank's study. Frank attempts to be casual and persuasive in tone, but Jonah can sense the uneasiness that undoubtedly has plagued Frank for most of his life. Frank speaks in euphemisms and incomplete sentences. Finally he manages to communicate that he wants Jonah to become President of San Lorenzo in his place.

He says that he is uninterested in the $100,000 salary and that he would rather maintain his role as a technical advisor. He assures Jonah that no one will contend his ascent to the office, because nobody in San Lorenzo cares about being president and to do so would be against their religion. Then Frank begs Jonah to take the job because he cannot be a public spokesperson.

Frank recounts his childhood. All of his peers would make fun of him and thought that he was a loser because he worked so much at Jack's Hobby Shop. Frank expresses dismay at their misunderstanding of his actions. They thought he had been going to the hobby shop to build model cars all day, but he actually had been having an affair with Jack's wife. Frank blames his exhaustion during the day at school on this fact. He considers it the reason that he always fell asleep in class and never reached his full potential.

Pushing away those memories, Frank returns to the matter at hand, which is to get Jonah to agree to become president. Although Jonah expresses some concern, he begins to acquiesce to Frank's request. Frank tells him that the only catch is that Jonah should probably marry Mona if he becomes president, since the Books of Bokonon predict that the next president will marry her. Amazed that the woman of his dreams might marry him, Jonah agrees to Frank's request.

Frank brings Mona to the study and leaves her with Jonah, who feels extremely nervous around her. She senses his uneasiness and assures him that he cannot make a mistake (a common greeting among Bokononists to shy people). When this does not help his nerves, she asks him if he would like to participate in boko–maru to see if that will help him talk to her. Jonah agrees, and despite his long sexual history with several women, he has never experienced such a soul–wrenching, sensual practice as boko–maru. After they finish, Jonah is on the verge of tears. He professes his deep love for Mona, who calmly reciprocates. When Jonah asks if Mona loves anyone else, she replies that she loves everyone and practices boko–maru with everyone, just as the Books of Bokonon say she should. When Jonah expresses dismay at this revelation and tries to restrain her to only loving and boko–maruing with him, she declares him a "sin–wat" and argues that to do so would be against her religion. She starts to dump him, but then he agrees that she can share her love with everyone. He also asks to be a part of her religion. He tells her that he loves her, and she again reciprocates.

Analysis

Frank is like his father in his desire to avoid human responsibility. He is willing to give up a large salary and marriage to the most beautiful woman on San Lorenzo in order to maintain his life as a behind–the–scenes technician. Frank has not recovered from his childhood wounds, and he therefore cannot see past his childish desires. It seems that he wants to remain in the lifestyle he built in Ilium in his adolescence, where he was able to create and manipulate a world to his liking without worrying about what others thought of him or his talents. Again, he serves of an example of a powerful man who is unable to help humanity because he does not care about or understand people.

Mona says Frank does not care about marrying her because he is still in love with the wife of Jack the Hobby Shop owner. Aside from the negative feelings of nervousness and fear, Frank has not exhibited any other human emotions. The idea of him being in love with her creates a series of questions about the nature of their relationship and their status as a couple, but the novel does not offer any insight into the situation. It is unclear whether his "love" for her is actually love or a manifestation of the same type of lust that Jonah mislabels as love. Obviously Frank left her when he moved from Ilium, so their relationship may not have been particularly strong. It is significant that in the end, all of these possibilities are complete speculation. It may be best for the reader to follow Bokonon's advice as explained by Julian Castle: do not to try to understand, but simply pretend to understand.

Jonah accepts the presidency because of his lust for Mona and power. He tries to believe that he will be a fair and effective leader, but there is no reason for him to be any more successful than any of San Lorenzo's other leaders. He has no ties to the island and is not even a member of the Bokononist religion, so he has no frame of reference from which to work in the best interest of the people. Jonah does not seem to realize that good intentions are not enough, and he has not internalized Bokonon's teaching that all human pursuits are useless.

Jonah's interest in serving as San Lorenzo's president is also based on his belief that she is his soul mate. Unfortunately, his desire to restrain Mona from practicing boko–maru shows that he does not understand her or her beliefs, and therefore he has no good grounds on which to love her. He accepts her love of others only because he does not want to lose it himself, but he would not have done so without her ultimatum. This scenario is interesting for its suggestion of a criticism of monogamy. The practice of boko–maru, while not sexual, is extremely intimate. The idea of sharing that pleasure with any and all people seems wrong to Jonah; it seems to violate the principle of monogamous intimacy. But through the premise that spiritual love may be shared, this physical practice becomes acceptable, which leaves the reader to question whether other physical practices should be considered acceptable under certain spiritual principles.

The lies that Jonah reads in the Books of Bokonon are of a piece with childhood stories and various myths about the origins of the planets and the moon. The Bokononist version provides a distinct feeling of mysticism. Bokonon does not care how strange the myth is, because he is not trying to fool any of his followers. He is secure enough in his lies and in the people's willingness to believe them that he will even write in his own religious texts that everything he preaches is a lie. The result, regardless, is that he has acquired a following among all of the people of San Lorenzo, even among those who have immigrated to the island. This religion offers people of the world's contemporary faiths a reason to consider whether their own religions include obvious lies that are accepted as such for the sake of some other purpose.

# Summary and Analysis of Chapters 94–110

The next morning, Jonah and Frank travel to Papa Monzano's castle to visit him at his deathbed. The castle was built by Tum–bumwa. As they reach the palace gate, Jonah notices a huge iron hook. The sign on it says that it is reserved for Bokonon himself, and for a moment Jonah sees himself as a great emancipator who will tear down that hook and allow the people to practice Bokononism freely.

When they arrive at the castle, they wait in an anteroom. While they wait, Jonah meets Dr. Vox Humana, a Christian minister who is there to administer Papa's last rites. He has with him a chicken and a butcher knife, which he says are his adaptations of Christian ritual––since he has not had sufficient opportunity to learn about more traditional practices. After briefly chatting with Dr. Humana, Frank and Jonah are allowed to see Papa. His bed is the lifeboat of Bokonon's old ship, the Lady's Slipper. Papa is shirtless, and on his heaving chest is a pendant containing a piece of ice–nine. Papa attempts to say good–bye to Frank, and he encourages Jonah to kill Bokonon when he becomes president. Papa asserts that science is the only magic that works, and he does not want his people to learn Bokononism anymore. Then he asks for his last rites. When Dr. Humana enters, Papa demands he leave. Papa reveals himself as a devout Bokononist after all, and he demands that someone administer the religion's rites to him in his last moments.

Dr. Koenigswald agrees to administer the Bokononist last rites, although he has never done so before and is not a Bokononist himself. Jonah asks Koenigswald if doing so will violate his beliefs as a scientist, and he replies that he is not a very good scientist because he will do anything to make a human feel better, even if it is unscientific. The doctor and Papa place themselves in the position of boko–maru, and they begin the responsive reading of the last rites.

Although Papa does not die in that moment, Frank and Jonah discuss how to announce Jonah's ascension to the office of president. They agree that he will do it that day at the Hundred Martyrs to Democracy ceremony, though Frank has little to offer in terms of that decision and has already begun to retreat into his shell again. Jonah prepares a humble and hopeful speech for the occasion and makes sure everyone is invited, even the Castles. At the ceremony, traditional San Lorenzan dishes are prepared, and the guests all have a choice of Pepsi or acetone rum as their beverage. H. Lowe Crosby is the only guest drinking the rum, and he and Hazel delight in the series of cardboard caricatures that have been set up in the harbor for the San Lorenzan fighter pilots to shoot down during the ceremony. Among the caricatures are Mao, Hitler, Marx, Stalin, and Castro, and Crosby declares that almost every enemy that freedom ever had can be found in that water.

No one knows that Jonah is about to become president. He engages in small talk with the Crosbys and the Castles and then makes the mistake of eating an hors d'oeuvre, which makes him sick. He retreats to Papa's castle, and after relieving himself, finds himself face to face with Dr. Koenigswald. The doctor expresses alarm because Papa has taken whatever was in the pendant around his neck and is now as dead and stiff as a rock. When Jonah enters the room he can see that this is true, and when he taps Papa's body it makes the sound of a marimba. Papa has died of ice–nine. Dr. Koenigswald makes the mistake of touching Papa with his bare hands, and when he goes to wash his hands the water turns solid at his touch. He touches the tip of his tongue to the block of ice on his hands (curiosity kills the cat), and instantly, he freezes solid and falls to the ground.

Jonah runs to the door and screams for the servants to bring him the Hoenikkers. When they arrive, Jonah berates them about giving ice–nine to Papa and endangering humanity. None of the Hoenikkers has a response, but Newt almost immediately throws up from the gravity of the situation. Neither of the other Hoenikkers offers an opinion. Newt asks Frank if giving Papa ice–nine is the way he got his job. Frank ignores Newt and states that they need to clean up the mess. Angela tries to confront Frank for the recklessness of giving ice–nine to Papa, but he suddenly snaps. He yells that buying his job with ice–nine is no different from Angela buying her husband with it and Newt using it to buy a week at the Cape with Zinka. Then he leaves the room.

Analysis

John, at one point, considers inviting Bokonon to the announcement of his presidency, but then realizes that he will have to continue the tension between good and evil because he has nothing to offer the San Lorenzans if he takes away the drama of their religion. Although he has delusions of himself as a fair and wise ruler who will lift the San Lorenzans from their destitution, he cannot bring himself to take away the one thing that is good in their lives without providing a suitable replacement. He cannot improve on Papa's practice of persecuting Bokonon and those who practice its teachings. Again, reality betrays his hypocrisy: his love, Mona, is a devout Bokononist, and he is a budding member of the religion himself. This conflict of interest pits his public duties as president against his private beliefs. The absurdity of both promoting and suppressing Bokononism reinforces the theme of a character's inability to realize the complete futility of even the most sincere pursuits.

Although Papa makes Jonah promise that he will find Bokonon and wipe out the remnants of Bokononism on San Lorenzo, he demands a Bokononist priest to administer his last rites. Papa too expresses the tension in seeming to suppress something of which he approves. Papa apparently uses Bokononism himself to cope with the reality of living on San Lorenzo and viewing the destitution of his people every day. Although he heralds the benefits of science to Jonah, he is not prepared to accept science as the primary source of truth and comfort in his own life.

Jonah expresses concern that he cannot decide whether Mona's calm indifference is a representation of the highest form of female spirituality or a testament to her anesthetized existence as an addict of the xylophone, the cult of beauty, and boko–maru. He decides to believe the former, because Bokonon teaches that it is better to believe a lie of love than to cling to a bitter truth. Yet, his realization that Mona is not perfect is a huge step toward his acceptance of Bokononism. Before this realization, he is trapped in the basic lies of lust instead of the lofty lies of Bokononism, and this step occurs on the basis of a nugget of truth about Mona's imperfection.

Following his discovery of Papa, Jonah is shocked at the recklessness of the Hoenikker children. He does not recall that he also has exhibited very reckless behavior throughout the novel, from his relationship with Krebbs to his one–night stand with Sandra the prostitute. Nonetheless, his indignation at the Hoenikker children's behavior and their unresponsiveness shows the difficulty of ensuring that humanity will learn from its mistakes. All the Hoenikkers seem concerned about is that another thing in their lives has gone wrong, regardless of their responsibility for the event. Jonah is dismayed at what little hope there could be for humanity when men like Felix Hoenikker give playthings like ice–nine to children like Frank, Angela, and Newt, leaving the fate of humanity in such hands. And would anyone else do any better with an invention like ice–nine?

# Summary and Analysis of Chapters 111–127

When Felix returns, the Hoenikkers begin cleaning Papa's bedroom of all traces of ice–nine. They use brooms, blowtorches, dustpans, hotplates, and buckets to collect and melt down all the large pieces of ice–nine that fell onto the floor. They skim the floor with the blowtorch. They also decide to build a funeral pyre to dispose of Papa's and Dr. Koenigswald's bodies. During this process, the Hoenikkers share with Jonah the story of the night their father told them about ice–nine. He had been making the substance in saucepans all day, shifting the molecules and then melting the ice down again. When ice–nine is melted, it returns to the same harmless state as natural water. Felix decided to take a break before cleaning up and melting down the remnants of his experiments, but he died in his rocking chair before he could do so. The whole day he had been teasing his children with the idea of ice–nine, urging them to stretch their minds and telling them its essential properties to see if they could guess what it was. They later found their father dead. None of the three children can explain why they each took a piece of the ice–nine. For them it is not a matter of morality. It is a matter of fact. After cleaning and scheduling the funeral pyre, everyone heads to the ceremony in honor of the Hundred Martyrs.

At the ceremony, Horlick Minton makes a speech that portrays all people who die in war as murdered children. He argues that ceremonies such as the one they are all attending should focus on eliminating false celebrations of honor and patriotism. Horlick expresses his appreciation for a thrilling show, but he argues that the only way to justify such shows is to hold them in conjunction with real efforts to reduce the stupidity and viciousness of humankind. He tosses a wreath into the sea, and the San Lorenzan air force begins its mission to destroy the cardboard caricatures floating in the sea.

Unfortunately, one of the planes in the show catches fire and crashes into the rocks over Papa's castle. The castle begins to fall and crumble, and the chaos that follows claims the lives of the Mintons. In a few ground–moving, terrain–shaking moments, Papa's bed and body are swept into the sea. It does not take long for ice–nine to cover the world and set off a chain of ecological disasters that kill almost all of Earth's inhabitants. From that point on, tornadoes cover the skies like worms.

Jonah and Mona find an underground bomb shelter in Papa's oubliette, where they can survive for a while. During this time, Jonah realizes that his lust for Mona may be misplaced, seeing that their only attempt at sex is met with much sweating and frustration but not very much pleasure. Afterward, Mona expresses her disdain for the activity.

The tornadoes begin to subside, and Mona and Jonah decide to venture out of their hiding place to see what has happened to the rest of the world. At first they are amazed to see that there are no dead bodies scattered around the island, but then they find most of the old inhabitants on Mount McCabe. Each has lain down calmly and committed suicide with ice–nine at the suggestion of Bokonon. Mona laughs at Jonah's dismay at the San Lorenzans' fates. She asks Jonah if he would ever wish any of the poor San Lorenzans alive again. Then she kills herself with ice–nine.

H. Lowe, Hazel, and Newt find Jonah later, and though he does not remember, they say he was crying. They take him back to Frank's house, where they live for six months with most of the creature comforts they had known before. Because ice–nine has frozen all of the animals on the island, the survivors have a reliable food source that they can defrost whenever they are hungry. Water is made by melting pure ice–nine. Hazel spends her time sewing an American flag, H. Lowe works as their cook, Newt paints, and Frank spends his days playing with an ant farm he has created. Ants are the only animals that survive, because they figure out a way to melt ice–nine with their bodies to make water.

Frank builds a transmitter to send S.O.S. signals, while John writes the present novel. Frank believes that he has matured a great deal following the destruction of the world. He does not lack self–confidence as much, and he does not care about what others think of him. Jonah reminds him that he has also killed almost every living thing on Earth, and that there are far fewer people to be socially anxious around. Frank ignores his comment.

Newt and Jonah discuss their lost sex drives one day as they are driving the only taxi around the island, and they realize that sex is uninteresting now that the world is truly hopeless and not worth inhabiting. John spots Bokonon sitting on a rock writing the last of his religious books, and he stops to speak with the prophet. Bokonon's last book reveals that, if he were a younger man, he would write a history of humanity's stupidity. Then, he would lie on the ground and thumb his nose at God, right before committing suicide.

Analysis

The Hoenikkers' tale of how they got their father's ice–nine highlights the disconnection between science and moral thinking. None of the children considered the questions of whether they should take the ice–nine or whether it was theirs to take, and this thoughtlessness exemplifies the relationship between science and morality in the novel. Discoveries are made without concern for their ultimate effect on humanity, and they are lauded by the world as advancements without regard to the moral and other human implications of making use of the discoveries. Most people do not understand the implications of scientists' research. Thus, the moral question is never asked, and science is permitted to exist in a vacuum.

Horlick Minton's speech is an attempt to make a small impact on people's perceptions of war and patriotism. The Hundred Martyrs' deaths seem unnecessary, but because they died in the name of democracy, they are now national heroes. Patriotism is unmasked as one of the world's worst granfalloons, because it is one for which people are most willing to die.

Papa Monzano's voyage to the sea in Bokonon's golden lifeboat fulfills Bokononist prophecy. However, because of the negligence of Jonah and the Hoenikkers, it can be argued on either side that the fulfillment of this prophecy is either destiny or the result of an abuse of free will. Perhaps the people subconsciously enable Bokonon's prophecy through their repeated mishandling of ice–nine.

In the final sections of Bokonon's work, Bokonon criticizes man's need for reason in his life. His version of God's whimsical creation of man and man's subsequent request for a purpose clearly indicates that he believes that man's search for reason is self–imposed. God tells man that he can have the privilege of making up a reason for life. Bokonon writes that man may be angry at this existence, but telling God of his anger would be pointless because God would only laugh. There is also no deep meaning behind the destruction of the Earth. It is the product of an accident by stupid humans. Since Earth's destruction is no more accidental than Earth's creation, it should not be considered a tragedy, but merely the result of a series of unimportant events.

Hazel's desire to create an American flag is a commentary on humanity's inability to learn from its mistakes. Since San Lorenzo's discovery, different nations have been claiming it mainly for the sake of doing so, or being mistaken about it having any real value. At the end of the Earth, with no one there to fight her for it, Hazel somehow remains interested in laying claim to this worthless land mass in the name of a now presumably nonexistent nation.

Newt and Jonah realize that the whole point of life might be the perpetuation of the human race through reproduction. They cannot think of any reason for existence other than existence itself. Thus, all of humanity's attempts to define and discover the meaning of life are nothing more than a cat's cradle, a funny–looking string that has not become a cat or a cradle.

# Suggested Essay Questions

1. What does the narrator say made him "a Jonah"?
2. How did the stone angel in Marvin Breed's tombstone shop serve as a vin–dit for Jonah?
3. In Dr. Breed's opinion, what is the purpose of pure research? How does this purpose compare with other people's understanding of science and the work of Felix Hoenikker? Consider the viewpoints of Miss Pefko, Miss Faust, Marvin Breed, and Bokonon.
4. Discuss the role of the karass and the granfalloon in the execution of God's will in the novel. Use examples of both relationships to demonstrate whether one is more important than the other in communicating points about the nature of human relationships and love.
5. Analyze how fulfilling their desires, or at least attempting to do so, either did or did not bring happiness to Vonnegut's characters.
6. How is Felix Hoenikker innocent? How is he not innocent? To what extent does a scientist's treatment of his work and the people with whom he interacts involve moral issues? Can or should science be a totally amoral, even inhuman, pursuit?
7. One of the tenets of Bokononism is that all human pursuits are useless. Does Bokononism itself fall under this category? Why or why not? Do the basic principles of a religion or a political system function differently for the founders than for the followers?
8. Discuss "Papa" Monzano's decision to use ice–nine to commit suicide. Was it a good idea, and does it appear that he knew that his decision would lead to the destruction of the world?
9. The idea of Dynamic Tension is central to the survival of Bokononism. Define Dynamic Tension, show how Bokonon maintained it on San Lorenzo, and indicate whether its presence is really necessary for religion or for enjoying one's life.
10. The Hundred Martyrs of Democracy died before they had even had an opportunity to fight in the Second World War. Is their contribution to the war effort more or less important than that of other soldiers? Is it more or less important than that of Felix Hoenikker?
11. Individual control and destiny are often portrated as competing forces in the novel. In your opinion, which of these is more important in determining characters' plight in the novel? How is this discussion complicated by recognizing that Vonnegut, as author, makes the choices that control the characters and the plot? Does an author make every choice for himself, or is he ultimately constrained by factors such as making the narrative believable––as though even the author does not have full control over the novel?

# The Book of Jonah

Vonnegut draws parallels to the biblical Book of Jonah in *Cat's Cradle* as a way of supporting themes about the incomprehensibility of God's plan and the inability of man to resist destiny. In the Bible, Jonah lives near the city of Nazareth. God commands him to travel to another city named Nineveh to prophesy to the people their impending destruction if they do not change their sinful ways. Jonah, however, angrily resists. He attempts to flee to Tarshish on a ship, but God sends a storm to interrupt the voyage. The other shipmen are frightened and entreat their gods to save them in light of this disaster. They find Jonah asleep in the sides of the ship, and the shipmaster asks him to also pray to his god for salvation. Soon the shipmen discover that Jonah is the reason for their danger, and they decide to throw Jonah into the ocean at his suggestion. Jonah is then swallowed by an ocean creature, usually interpreted as a whale, and he survives in its belly for three days. He prays to God for his release, and Jonah is vomited from the mouth of the whale.

When he is released from the whale, again the Lord directs him to Nineveh. Jonah obeys and prophesies their destruction in forty days if they do not repent, so the people fast and wear sackcloth to show their penitence. Jonah, still an angry fellow, is unhappy at the idea of God saving the people of Nineveh, so he leaves the city and sits upon a hill to see whether God will destroy it or not. While he is sitting there, God causes a gourd to grow above his head so that he might have shade. Jonah is glad for this gourd, but God then causes a worm to kill the gourd and the sun beats upon Jonah's head (creating the joke that things are now too hot for the hot–headed man). Jonah wishes for death, because he believes it better for him to be dead than alive, and he is very angry that the gourd died. God confronts Jonah and asks why he values the gourd more than the people of Nineveh, since the people of Nineveh cannot distinguish between their right hand and their left hand.

The Book of Jonah has been important in theologians' interpretation of the ideas of destiny and God's will. Jonah is intent on defying God and following his own desires, but he is unable to resist God's divine plan. God used Jonah as he saw fit, and he remained unchanged by Jonah's desire to be uninvolved in the salvation of Nineveh. Further, it is important to note that although the people of Nineveh are sinful, they are given the opportunity to repent and gain salvation through the grace of God. Because the people of Nineveh were ignorant of their sin, God proclaimed them worthy of mercy as long as they chose to repent for their transgressions.

Most scholars believe the story of Jonah is fictitious because the idea of being swallowed by a whale seems so fantastic. Yet, there have been documented cases of humans being subject to similar plights, such as the seaman who was swallowed by a sperm whale in the 1900s near the Falkland Islands. Although he had damage to his skin and was unconscious when he was recovered, he managed to survive being inside the whale for three days.

Jonah is often interpreted as a figure for Christ, a view that was first proposed by Augustine. As Jesus would be, Jonah was taken from the world for three days and returned after that period with a message of salvation for the people.

# Author of ClassicNote and Sources

Kellee Patterson, author of ClassicNote. Completed on March 11, 2006, copyright held by GradeSaver.

Updated and revised Adam Kissel April 14, 2006. Copyright held by GradeSaver.

Schatt, Stanley. Kurt Vonnegut, Jr. Boston: Twayne, 1976.

Tanner, Tony. City of Words. New York: Harper &Row, 1971.

Goldsmith, David H. Kurt Vonnegut: Fantasies of Fire and Ice. Bowling Green, Ohio: Bowling Green University Popular Press, 1972.

Morse, Donald E. The Novels of Kurt Vonnegut: Imagining Being an American. Westport, CT: Praeger, 2003.

Klinkowitz, Jerome. Vonnegut in Fact: The Public Spokesmanship of Personal Fiction. Columbia: University of South Carolina Press, 1998.

Merill, Robert. Critical Essays on Kurt Vonnegut. Boston: G. K. Hall, 1990.

Vonnegut, Kurt. Cat's Cradle. New York: Delacourt Press, 1963.

Baker, Lyman A. "San Lorenzo Dialect &Bokononisms: A List of First Occurrences." 2003−02−27. 2006−01−26. <http://www.ksu.edu/english/baker/english287/sg−Vonnegut−CC_Bokonisms.htm>.

Jackson, Wayne. "Great Truths from the Book of Jonah." Christian Courier: Archives. 1999−04−12. 2006−03−03. <http://www.christiancourier.com/archives/jonah.htm>.

# Essay: Organized Religion in Kurt Vonnegut's Cats Cradle: See God? See Satan?

by Auvijit Chakder
May 11, 2004

"See the cat? See the cradle?" retorts the midget Newt in an attempt to explain the inspiration for a grotesque and confounding painting of his. This singular quote is the namesake for Kurt Vonnegut's novel *Cat's Cradle*, and embodies the leitmotif of this tongue–in–cheek canon on religion, sex, politics, and everything in between. In the years following its publication, Vonnegut's novel became fodder for the counterculture movement of the 1960's because it countered the restrictive societal norms of mainstream culture. Among the institutions he attacks throughout the novel, religion is the most conspicuous. Vonnegut dissects the very human inclination to have something to believe in, questioning not only the nature of organized religion, but its validity and role in society. Vonnegut creates a picturesque island named San Lorenzo, whose national religion is the work of a nihilistic poet. Vonnegut uses this religion, called "Bokononism", as a vehicle for the revelation (no pun intended) that religion is as substantial as a "cat's cradle."

Vonnegut introduces the "cat's cradle" as a metaphor for different interpretations of life. "A cat's cradle is nothing more than a bunch of X's between somebody's hands" (165) says Newt, who had been traumatized as a child by the sight of his father dangling such "tangles of string" (165) in his face. And though there is "no damn cat, and no damn cradle"(166) the "little kids look and look and look at all those X's (166). According to Newt's cradle metaphor, one sees what one wants to. "See the cat? See the cradle?" (179) Newt says in response to inquiries about his sister's seemingly perfect marriage and Jesus Christ, both of whom are not what they people may think they are. Here is the philosophy Vonnegut espouses throughout the novel. People tend to see what they want to, and read into what is there in reality. Religion is no exception to this.

Vonnegut creates a religion in order to question the role of faith in society and the validity of traditional religiooous assumptions. He first questions absolutes during a dialogue between the scientist Felix Hoenikker and a secretary, Miss Faust. "God is love" (55) claims the latter. "What is God? What is love?" (55) replies the former. According to the Books of Bokonon (the founder of Vonnegut's fictitious religion), one should "believe in the foma [harmless untruths] that make you brave and kind and healthy and happy" (i). To understand this assertion, one must take into account the Bokononist premise that "all religions are nothing but lies" (219). Thus, a "useful religion can be founded on lies"(6) so long as it inspires its followers to be "kind and healthy and happy." Miss Faust is content to believe in the Christian presumption that God is love without any physical proof "no matter what Dr. Hoenikker said"

(55). Yet, if this belief makes Miss Faust all those things aforementioned, her religion can be said to be "useful." This is her "cat's cradle." She takes into account the nature of the world and interprets it in light of Christianity.

Vonnegut later uses his fictitious religion to model how religion takes into account the nature of things, and interprets them based on assumptions. His vehicle for this point is the cosmogony found in the Books of Bokonon. In it, Bokonon observes the planetary orbits. The assumptions that a follower of Bokononism must make is that the sun is a living entity and has a name, "Borasisi", and that he somehow produced children with another living entity, the moon, whose name is "Pabu." Bokonon then relates a story of how Pabu bore unsatisfactory children (who became the planets who orbit "at safe distance" (191)) and Pabu's exile to live with her "favorite child" who was earth. Bokonon claims that earth was her favorite because it harbored people who "looked up at her and loved her and sympathized" (191). Don't all religions make claims such as the ones that Vonnegut presents in this cosmogony? This is where the principle if faith comes from. We cannot prove the claims that many religions make, yet people still have faith that they are true. The main difference between Bokononist cosmogony and that of more mainstream religion is that Bokonon is quick to admit that all of it is "foma" or "harmless lies." Vonnegut intentionally does this in order for us to see how strange our religion would seem if we were approaching it for the first time. What proof is there that all religions do not consist of "foma," carefully constructed to make people more orderly and happy? This is Vonnegut's ultimate point, and one that attracts many to the book.

Vonnegut also parallels religion's attempts to explain the origin of the earth with his Creation story. "In the beginning," he writes (referencing the book of Genesis) "God created the earth and looked upon it with his cosmic loneliness" (265). God then "created every living creature that now moveth" (265) out of mud. One of these creatures was Man. Man then inquired what the purpose of this creation was. God's answer is "I leave it to you to think of one for all this" (265). Vonnegut is playing with the human belief that there must be a purpose for everything. This is what leads people to espouse religious beliefs in the first place. Religious people have tried for centuries to determine "the reason for all this" and have developed elaborate answers. Yet, if we are to believe Bokonon, all of it is "foma" and life doesn't require a purpose.

Religion, as Vonnegut would have it, has probably exceeded its authority in a world where so many people are hindered by their creed. If we are to assume that all religions are "foma", religion serves its most useful purpose so long as it does not overstep its boundaries. Vonnegut is, in essence saying that religion is not to be taken too seriously. For all the faith people invest in their beliefs, religion can never be proven. Vonnegut wants the reader to ask, what if religion is nothing but lies? With Vonnegut, one must anticipate the next question. Does it really matter if religions are made up of lies so long as they make people "brave and kind and healthy and happy"? So long as we force ourselves to see what isn't there, and attempt to explain what is, the world will always be tangled up in a "cat's cradle."

# Quiz 1

1. **What was Felix Hoenikker's profession?**
   A. Writer
   B. Bartender
   C. Scientist
   D. Theologian

2. **What was the name of Newt's fiancee?**
   A. Enza
   B. Zinka
   C. Emily
   D. Angela

3. **What is the narrator's adopted name?**
   A. Bokonon
   B. Sam
   C. John
   D. Jonah

4. **What was the title of the narrator's novel?**
   A. The Heroes of the Atomic Bomb
   B. The Day the World Ended
   C. The Hoenikkers: A History
   D. Cat's Cradle

5. **How did the narrator meet Newt?**
   A. They never met.
   B. They belonged to the same fraternity.
   C. They went to medical school together.
   D. He met him in a bar in Ilium.

6. **What is a karass?**
   A. A traditional cloth worn by Bokononists
   B. A team of individuals who do God's will
   C. A person who rejects Bokononism
   D. A biological weapon

7. **What was Felix Hoenikker's supervisor's name?**
    A. Dr. Breed
    B. Dr. Faust
    C. Bokonon
    D. Frank

8. **Where do most Bokononists live?**
    A. Ilium, NY
    B. Near the site of the Manhattan Project
    C. An island off the coast of Germany
    D. The Republic of San Lorenzo

9. **What is a cat's cradle?**
    A. A type of drink
    B. A secret handshake from Newt's fraternity
    C. A shape made with string
    D. A biological weapon

10. **How old was Angela on the day the atomic bomb was dropped?**
    A. Thirty
    B. Sixteen
    C. Six
    D. Twenty–two

11. **What did scientists discover as the secret of life, according to the bartender in Ilium?**
    A. Protein
    B. The atomic bomb
    C. Faith
    D. Molecular restructuring

12. **What kind of drink did the bartender in Ilium make for the Japanese bum who entered his bar on the day the bomb was dropped?**
    A. Shirley Temple
    B. End of the World Delight
    C. Moonshine
    D. Vodka Tonic

13. **Who did the townspeople in Ilium think was the father of Emily Hoenikker's children?**
    A. Dr. Breed
    B. The bartender whom Jonah met
    C. Felix
    D. Dr. Breed's son

14. **Why did Emily die when giving birth to Newt?**
    A. She was diabetic and went into shock
    B. She lost too much blood
    C. She did not recover from the anesthesia
    D. She was in a car accident that damaged her pelvis

15. **What does Dr. Breed think is a scientist's primary purpose?**
    A. To make his country more powerful than any other
    B. To increase knowledge
    C. To make people more comfortable
    D. To save lives

16. **Why was ice-nine developed?**
    A. So Felix could retire
    B. So America could use it to threaten Russia
    C. So Angela could find a husband
    D. So Marines would not have to wade through mud

17. **What did Dr. Breed call normal ice?**
    A. Solid water
    B. Frozen water
    C. Old ice
    D. Ice-one

18. **What present does Dr. Breed give to the Girl Pool each Christmas?**
    A. Wreaths
    B. Chocolate bars
    C. Candy canes
    D. Money

19. **Who is Miss Faust?**
    A. Bokonon's wife
    B. Jonah's secretary
    C. Felix's secretary
    D. Dr. Breed's secretary

20. **What is the melting point of ice–nine?**
    A. Below 0 degrees Farenheit
    B. Between 0 and 50 degrees Farenheit
    C. Above 100 degrees Farenheit
    D. Between 50 and 100 degrees Farenheit

21. **What happened to the ice–nine Felix created after his death?**
    A. It was buried with him
    B. His children split it up
    C. The government claimed it
    D. His children threw it away

22. **When and where did Felix Hoenikker die?**
    A. On Christmas in Cape Cod
    B. On New Year's Day in Ilium
    C. On his birthday in San Lorenzo
    D. On Valentine's Day in a plane crash

23. **What was Felix Hoenikker's response to the phrase "God is love?"**
    A. "Science is love."
    B. "What is God? What is love?"
    C. "I am a Bokononist."
    D. "I don't believe in God."

24. **What kind of memorial did Emily Hoenikker's children leave her?**
    A. A wooden cross
    B. A donation to an anti–war foundation
    C. A small cube
    D. A very large alabaster structure

25. **Who owned the tombstone store in Ilium?**
    A. Newt Hoenikker
    B. Frank Hoenikker
    C. Miss Faust
    D. Marvin Breed, Dr. Asa Breed's brother

# Quiz 1 Answer Key

1. **(C)** Scientist
2. **(B)** Zinka
3. **(D)** Jonah
4. **(B)** The Day the World Ended
5. **(B)** They belonged to the same fraternity.
6. **(B)** A team of individuals who do God's will
7. **(A)** Dr. Breed
8. **(D)** The Republic of San Lorenzo
9. **(C)** A shape made with string
10. **(D)** Twenty–two
11. **(A)** Protein
12. **(B)** End of the World Delight
13. **(A)** Dr. Breed
14. **(D)** She was in a car accident that damaged her pelvis
15. **(B)** To increase knowledge
16. **(D)** So Marines would not have to wade through mud
17. **(D)** Ice–one
18. **(B)** Chocolate bars
19. **(D)** Dr. Breed's secretary
20. **(C)** Above 100 degrees Farenheit
21. **(B)** His children split it up
22. **(A)** On Christmas in Cape Cod
23. **(B)** "What is God? What is love?"
24. **(D)** A very large alabaster structure
25. **(D)** Marvin Breed, Dr. Asa Breed's brother

# Quiz 2

1. **Who was the stone angel in the tombstone store made for?**
   A. The taxi driver
   B. Frank Hoenikker
   C. Emily Hoenikker
   D. One of Jonah's ancestors

2. **What was Philip Castle's book called?**
   A. Bokononist Thought and the Cold War
   B. San Lorenzo: The Land, the History, the People
   C. The Biography of Mona Monzano
   D. Great Hoosiers of the 20th Century

3. **What first attracted Jonah to the supplement about San Lorenzo?**
   A. His own picture on the cover
   B. "Papa" Monzano's picture on the cover
   C. Mona Monzano's picture on the cover
   D. Frank Hoenikker's picture on the cover

4. **How did Jonah meet the Mintons?**
   A. They stayed in his apartment while he was in Ilium
   B. They owned the hobby shop where Frank used to work
   C. They were mourning in the cemetery in Ilium
   D. They were his seatmates on the plane to San Lorenzo

5. **What was written on the note Sherman Krebbs left around the neck of Jonah's dead cat?**
   A. A threatening letter
   B. A hospital bill
   C. The word "meow"
   D. A haiku

6. **What was H. Lowe Crosby's profession?**
   A. Bicycle maker
   B. Bartender
   C. Ambassador
   D. Pilot

7. **Where did Jonah meet Angela Hoenikker?**
    A. He cannot remember
    B. On the plane to San Lorenzo
    C. In Ilium at her mother's gravesite
    D. At home with her husband in Indianapolis

8. **On whose theory of Dynamic Tension did Bokonon base his religion?**
    A. Charles Atlas
    B. Dr. Breed
    C. Felix Hoenikker
    D. "Papa" Monzano

9. **What was the name of Bokonon's first ship?**
    A. Lady's Slipper
    B. Maiden of the Sea
    C. Johnson's Vessel
    D. Fate's Ferry

10. **With whom did Bokonon first arrive on San Lorenzo?**
    A. Frank Hoenikker
    B. Earl McCabe
    C. "Papa" Monzano
    D. Mona Monzano

11. **What was San Lorenzo's greatest natural resource?**
    A. It had no natural resources
    B. Diamonds
    C. Oil
    D. Gold

12. **Whom did Angela marry?**
    A. Bokonon
    B. Harrison Conners
    C. Jonah
    D. Dr. Breed's son

### 13. **Where was Newt and Zinka's love nest?**
   A. His father's house on Cape Cod
   B. His sister's house in Indianapolis
   C. Her apartment in Russia
   D. The Casa Mona in San Lorenzo

### 14. **To what tune is the San Lorenzan national anthem sung?**
   A. Home on the Range
   B. All Shook Up
   C. Fair Harvard
   D. Stars and Stripes Forever

### 15. **What instrument does Mona Monzano play?**
   A. Violin
   B. Clarinet
   C. Recorder
   D. Xylophone

### 16. **What is the primary method of punishment on San Lorenzo?**
   A. The hook
   B. The guillotine
   C. The electric chair
   D. The gallows

### 17. **What is the currency of San Lorenzo?**
   A. Rubles
   B. Dollars
   C. Corporals
   D. Pesos

### 18. **Who were the Hundred Martyrs to Democracy?**
   A. San Lorenzan volunteers to the Second World War
   B. The first people who died on the hook
   C. Villagers killed by Tum–bumwa
   D. Bokononism's first hundred followers

### 19. Why did Tum-wumba kill 700 San Lorenzans?
A. For substandard zeal
B. For being Bokononists
C. For stealing
D. For foot play

### 20. What was Philip Castle's hotel called?
A. Bokononist's Retreat
B. Castle's Castle
C. Casa Mona
D. San Lorenzo Hilton

### 21. Why did Claire Minton say Philip Castle would never marry Mona Monzano?
A. It was against his religion to marry
B. He was not in love with her
C. He was a homosexual
D. He would die before their wedding

### 22. How did the bubonic plague reach the island of San Lorenzo?
A. Ice-nine attracted the plague virus
B. A ship carrying wicker furniture crashed into the island, bringing rats
C. Earl McCabe used it as a weapon to oppress the island's people
D. A mad scientist released the plague as an experiment on the island's people

### 23. Why did Julian Castle mention Jesus?
A. To keep his voice box working
B. To counter his son's argument for Bokononism
C. To express his deep faith
D. To offer hope to the San Lorenzans

### 24. What did Julian Castle do with Newt's painting of a cat's cradle?
A. He bought it for Jonah
B. He put it on display in his son's hotel
C. He threw it into the waterfall
D. He drew his own version of the painting

## 25. **Why did Philip Castle build Casa Mona?**

A. Because he thought it would be really profitable

B. Because it was either that or become a hermit

C. Because Mona asked him to

D. Because his father wanted him to

# Quiz 2 Answer Key

1. **(D)** One of Jonah's ancestors
2. **(B)** San Lorenzo: The Land, the History, the People
3. **(C)** Mona Monzano's picture on the cover
4. **(D)** They were his seatmates on the plane to San Lorenzo
5. **(C)** The word "meow"
6. **(A)** Bicycle maker
7. **(B)** On the plane to San Lorenzo
8. **(A)** Charles Atlas
9. **(A)** Lady's Slipper
10. **(B)** Earl McCabe
11. **(A)** It had no natural resources
12. **(B)** Harrison Conners
13. **(A)** His father's house on Cape Cod
14. **(A)** Home on the Range
15. **(D)** Xylophone
16. **(A)** The hook
17. **(C)** Corporals
18. **(A)** San Lorenzan volunteers to the Second World War
19. **(A)** For substandard zeal
20. **(C)** Casa Mona
21. **(C)** He was a homosexual
22. **(B)** A ship carrying wicker furniture crashed into the island, bringing rats
23. **(A)** To keep his voice box working
24. **(C)** He threw it into the waterfall
25. **(B)** Because it was either that or become a hermit

# Quiz 3

1. **Of what religion are all residents of the island of San Lorenzo?**
   A. Christianity
   B. Atheism
   C. Bokononism
   D. Islam

2. **What did Angela Hoenikker use as evidence to argue that her father was underappreciated?**
   A. His tombstone was much smaller than her mother's
   B. He was never made a Saint
   C. He was paid thousands less than Dr. Breed
   D. He never won the Nobel Prize

3. **Why was Angela Hoenikker upset when she was visiting San Lorenzo, according to Newt?**
   A. She felt bad about losing touch with Frank for all those years
   B. She was shocked at the plight of the San Lorenzans
   C. Her husband was cheating on her
   D. She was unhappy with her career

4. **What is Bokonon's religion based on?**
   A. Science
   B. The cosmos
   C. Lies
   D. Truth

5. **What favor did Frank want from Jonah?**
   A. He wanted Jonah to take Angela and Newt back to the States
   B. He wanted Jonah to assume Bokonon's role after Bokonon died
   C. He wanted Jonah to be the American Ambassador to San Lorenzo
   D. He wanted Jonah to take his place as the next President

6. **How much money does the President of San Lorenzo make?**
   A. Nothing. It is a volunteer position.
   B. $5,000
   C. $28,000
   D. $100,000

7. **What convinced Jonah to become President of San Lorenzo?**
    A. He would be paid a large sum of money
    B. He would get to save the people of the island
    C. He would get to marry Mona
    D. He would not have to return to the States

8. **What did Angela and Newt keep in their thermoses?**
    A. Ice–nine
    B. Mud
    C. Soup
    D. Pictures of their father

9. **Why did Dr. Koenigswald become a physician on San Lorenzo?**
    A. He wanted to make a lot of money off the illnesses of the San Lorenzans
    B. As penance for his role in Auschwitz
    C. His mother had died from the bubonic plague
    D. Julian Castle asked him to join his practice

10. **What was the highest mountain on San Lorenzo?**
    A. Mount St. Helen
    B. Lorenzo's Peak
    C. Bokonon's cave
    D. Mount McCabe

11. **What is a duprass?**
    A. A new convert to Bokononism
    B. A type of plant
    C. A karass made up of two people
    D. A lie told by a ruler to the ruled

12. **Who was the first person to die from ice–nine?**
    A. Dr. Koenigswald
    B. Felix Hoenikker
    C. "Papa" Monzano
    D. Mona Monzano

## 13. What did Newt do when he saw Papa Monzano's corpse?

A. He cried

B. He vomited

C. He touched the corpse and died himself

D. He passed out

## 14. When was Jonah going to anounce his ascension to the presidency?

A. The day of the celebration of the Hundred Martyrs to Democracy

B. After Newt's birthday

C. After Papa died

D. After Frank announced his engagement to Mona

## 15. Who built Papa's castle?

A. Julian Castle's grandfather

B. Bokonon

C. Tum−bumwa

D. The Spanish conquerors of the island

## 16. What was Papa's bed made from?

A. Bokonon's old lifeboat

B. Ice

C. Marble quarried from the hills

D. Foam rubber

## 17. What did Hazel tell Hoosiers to call her?

A. Mr. Crosby

B. Mom

C. Crazy Hazel

D. Hoosier Lady

## 18. What is the one aspect of progess that interests the people of San Lorenzo?

A. Ice−nine

B. The atomic bomb

C. Luxury jets

D. The electric guitar

19. **What did Frank want to use to eliminate the remains of Papa Monzano and Dr. Koenigswald?**
    A. Pool–pah
    B. Dynamite
    C. A blowtorch
    D. Water

20. **What did Felix Hoenikker write on the bottle of ice–nine he showed his children?**
    A. Ice–Nine
    B. Cyanide
    C. Meow
    D. Danger!

21. **Where did the Hoenikkers put their dead dog?**
    A. Under the house
    B. In the oven
    C. On Papa's doorstep
    D. In the woods

22. **What was written on Horlick Minton's wreath?**
    A. Pro Patria
    B. Long Live Bokonon
    C. U.S.S.R.
    D. San Lorenzo

23. **Who was Dr. Vox Humana?**
    A. A Christian minister
    B. A pediatrician
    C. An organist
    D. A college professor

24. **What is a sin–wat?**
    A. A person who wants one person's love all to himself
    B. A person who boko–marus with Mona
    C. A person who is killed on the hook
    D. A person who works for Papa

25. **What does Papa think is the only magic that works?**
   A. Voodoo
   B. Science
   C. Love
   D. Bokononism

# Quiz 3 Answer Key

1. **(C)** Bokononism
2. **(C)** He was paid thousands less than Dr. Breed
3. **(C)** Her husband was cheating on her
4. **(C)** Lies
5. **(D)** He wanted Jonah to take his place as the next President
6. **(D)** $100,000
7. **(C)** He would get to marry Mona
8. **(A)** Ice–nine
9. **(B)** As penance for his role in Auschwitz
10. **(D)** Mount McCabe
11. **(C)** A karass made up of two people
12. **(C)** "Papa" Monzano
13. **(B)** He vomited
14. **(A)** The day of the celebration of the Hundred Martyrs to Democracy
15. **(C)** Tum–bumwa
16. **(A)** Bokonon's old lifeboat
17. **(B)** Mom
18. **(D)** The electric guitar
19. **(C)** A blowtorch
20. **(D)** Danger!
21. **(B)** In the oven
22. **(A)** Pro Patria
23. **(A)** A Christian minister
24. **(A)** A person who wants one person's love all to himself
25. **(B)** Science

# Quiz 4

1. **Who was Frank in love with?**
   A. Philip Castle
   B. Miss Pefko
   C. Jack's wife
   D. Mona

2. **How did the Mintons die?**
   A. They were crushed by a castle
   B. They were put on the hook
   C. They took ice–nine
   D. They were hit by a jet plane

3. **What did the ice–nine dishrag feel like to Newt?**
   A. A wet rag
   B. A paper–like wad
   C. A reticule
   D. A rock

4. **In what language did Horlick give most of his speech?**
   A. San Lorenzan English
   B. Yiddish
   C. Spanish
   D. American English

5. **What poem did Horlick Minton recite?**
   A. Four Quartets
   B. The Broken Hero
   C. Leaves of Grass
   D. Spoon River Anthology

6. **What does Pro Patria mean?**
   A. For one's father
   B. For one's mother
   C. For one's country
   D. For oneself

7. **What caused Papa's castle to fall?**
   A. An earthquake
   B. A tornado
   C. A jet plane
   D. A bulldozer

8. **What did the Crosbys yell at the tornado to protect themselves?**
   A. All hail Bokonon!
   B. God help us!
   C. Foma!
   D. American! American!

9. **Where did Jonah and Mona find refuge?**
   A. On Mount McCabe
   B. In a treehouse
   C. At the airport
   D. In Papa's oubliette

10. **What did Mona think of sex?**
    A. She thought it was necessary
    B. She never had sex
    C. She did not like it
    D. She loved it

11. **What was the climate of Earth after ice–nine froze the oceans?**
    A. Cold and humid
    B. Hot and dry
    C. Cold and dry
    D. Hot and humid

12. **From what did most San Lorenzans die after ice–nine froze the oceans?**
    A. Suicide
    B. Gunshot wounds
    C. Tornadoes
    D. Earthquakes

13. **What did Mona do when she found the dead San Lorenzans?**
    A. She passed out
    B. She sang
    C. She cried
    D. She laughed

14. **Who found Jonah after Mona died?**
    A. Newt and Frank
    B. The Crosbys and Frank
    C. Frank, Newt, and the Crosbys
    D. The Crosbys and Newt

15. **What did Frank paint on the island's black taxi?**
    A. "Long Live San Lorenzo"
    B. "Illegitimum Non Carborundum"
    C. "U.S.A."
    D. "S.O.S."

16. **How long did it take Jonah to write Cat's Cradle?**
    A. A decade
    B. Two years
    C. Six months
    D. Three weeks

17. **What did Hazel make after ice-nine froze the oceans?**
    A. An American flag
    B. An ant farm
    C. A sweater for Newt
    D. A monument for the San Lorenzans

18. **What killed Angela?**
    A. She played her clarinet, even though it was covered in ice-nine
    B. She was struck by "Papa's" Castle
    C. She was hit by a tornado
    D. Newt murdered her

19. **What did Hazel say was the benefit of the freezing of the oceans?**
    A. No Communists
    B. No mosquitoes
    C. No Bokononists
    D. No San Lorenzans

20. **Who cooked for the refugees?**
    A. Newt
    B. H. Lowe
    C. Jonah
    D. Hazel

21. **What did Frank think was the reason for ants' success?**
    A. They are small
    B. They cooperate
    C. They are evolving
    D. God left them alone

22. **What was Newt's Mongoloid friend named?**
    A. Will
    B. Zinka
    C. Myrna
    D. Janice

23. **What did Jonah call a depressing religion?**
    A. Christianity
    B. Science
    C. Bokononism
    D. Islam

24. **What was Bokonon doing when Jonah met him?**
    A. Raiding Papa's Castle
    B. Writing his last "Book"
    C. Dancing in the tornadoes
    D. Sleeping in the remnants of the Casa Mona

25. **What is the moral of Cat's Cradle as written by Jonah?**
    A. Humans are the most important creatures on Earth
    B. The innocent will be rewarded
    C. Men can orchestrate their fates
    D. Life has no purpose

# Quiz 4 Answer Key

1. **(C)** Jack's wife
2. **(A)** They were crushed by a castle
3. **(C)** A reticule
4. **(D)** American English
5. **(D)** Spoon River Anthology
6. **(C)** For one's country
7. **(C)** A jet plane
8. **(D)** American! American!
9. **(D)** In Papa's oubliette
10. **(C)** She did not like it
11. **(B)** Hot and dry
12. **(A)** Suicide
13. **(D)** She laughed
14. **(D)** The Crosbys and Newt
15. **(C)** "U.S.A."
16. **(C)** Six months
17. **(A)** An American flag
18. **(A)** She played her clarinet, even though it was covered in ice–nine
19. **(B)** No mosquitoes
20. **(B)** H. Lowe
21. **(B)** They cooperate
22. **(C)** Myrna
23. **(C)** Bokononism
24. **(B)** Writing his last "Book"
25. **(D)** Life has no purpose

# ClassicNotes

## GradeSaver™

*Getting you the grade since 1999*™

## Other ClassicNotes from GradeSaver™

1984
Absalom, Absalom
Adam Bede
The Adventures of Augie
  March
The Adventures of
  Huckleberry Finn
The Adventures of Tom
  Sawyer
The Aeneid
Agamemnon
The Age of Innocence
Alice in Wonderland
All My Sons
All Quiet on the Western
  Front
All the King's Men
All the Pretty Horses
The Ambassadors
American Beauty
Angela's Ashes
Animal Farm
Anna Karenina
Antigone
Antony and Cleopatra
Aristotle's Ethics
Aristotle's Poetics
Aristotle's Politics
As I Lay Dying
As You Like It
The Awakening
Babbitt
The Bacchae
Bartleby the Scrivener
The Bean Trees
The Bell Jar

Beloved
Benito Cereno
Beowulf
Billy Budd
Black Boy
Bleak House
Bluest Eye
Brave New World
Breakfast at Tiffany's
Call of the Wild
Candide
The Canterbury Tales
Cat's Cradle
Catch-22
The Catcher in the Rye
The Caucasian Chalk
  Circle
The Cherry Orchard
The Chosen
A Christmas Carol
Chronicle of a Death
  Foretold
Civil Disobedience
Civilization and Its
  Discontents
A Clockwork Orange
The Color of Water
The Color Purple
Comedy of Errors
Communist Manifesto
A Confederacy of
  Dunces
Connecticut Yankee in
  King Arthur's Court
Coriolanus

The Count of Monte
  Cristo
Crime and Punishment
The Crucible
Cry, the Beloved
  Country
The Crying of Lot 49
Cymbeline
Daisy Miller
Death in Venice
Death of a Salesman
The Death of Ivan Ilych
Democracy in America
Devil in a Blue Dress
The Diary of Anne Frank
Disgrace
Divine Comedy-I:
  Inferno
A Doll's House
Don Quixote Book I
Don Quixote Book II
Dr. Faustus
Dr. Jekyll and Mr. Hyde
Dracula
Dubliners
East of Eden
Emma
Ender's Game
Endgame
Ethan Frome
The Eumenides
Everything is Illuminated
Fahrenheit 451
The Fall of the House of
  Usher
Farewell to Arms

For our full list of over 250 Study Guides, Quizzes,
Sample College Application Essays, Literature Essays and E-texts, visit:

**www.gradesaver.com**

# ClassicNotes

## GradeSaver™

*Getting you the grade since 1999*™

## Other ClassicNotes from GradeSaver™

The Federalist Papers
For Whom the Bell Tolls
The Fountainhead
Frankenstein
Franny and Zooey
Glass Menagerie
The God of Small Things
The Grapes of Wrath
Great Expectations
The Great Gatsby
Hamlet
The Handmaid's Tale
Hard Times
Heart of Darkness
Hedda Gabler
Henry IV (Pirandello)
Henry IV Part 1
Henry IV Part 2
Henry V
The Hobbit
Homo Faber
House of Mirth
House of the Seven
    Gables
The House of the Spirits
House on Mango Street
Howards End
A Hunger Artist
I Know Why the Caged
    Bird Sings
An Ideal Husband
Iliad
The Importance of Being
    Earnest
In Our Time
Inherit the Wind

Invisible Man
The Island of Dr. Moreau
Jane Eyre
Jazz
The Joy Luck Club
Julius Caesar
Jungle of Cities
Kidnapped
King Lear
Last of the Mohicans
Leviathan
Libation Bearers
The Lion, the Witch and
    the Wardrobe
Lolita
Long Day's Journey Into
    Night
Lord Jim
Lord of the Flies
The Lord of the Rings:
    The Fellowship of the
    Ring
The Lord of the Rings:
    The Return of the
    King
The Lord of the Rings:
    The Two Towers
A Lost Lady
The Love Song of J.
    Alfred Prufrock
Lucy
Macbeth
Madame Bovary
Manhattan Transfer
Mansfield Park
MAUS

The Mayor of
    Casterbridge
Measure for Measure
Medea
Merchant of Venice
Metamorphoses
The Metamorphosis
Middlemarch
Midsummer Night's
    Dream
Moby Dick
Moll Flanders
Mother Courage and Her
    Children
Mrs. Dalloway
Much Ado About
    Nothing
My Antonia
Native Son
Night
No Exit
Notes from Underground
O Pioneers
The Odyssey
Oedipus Rex / Oedipus
    the King
Of Mice and Men
The Old Man and the Sea
On Liberty
One Day in the Life of
    Ivan Denisovich
One Flew Over the
    Cuckoo's Nest
One Hundred Years of
    Solitude
Oroonoko

For our full list of over 250 Study Guides, Quizzes,
Sample College Application Essays, Literature Essays and E-texts, visit:

**www.gradesaver.com**

# ClassicNotes

# GradeSaver™

*Getting you the grade since 1999*™

## Other ClassicNotes from GradeSaver™

Othello
Our Town
Pale Fire
Paradise Lost
A Passage to India
The Pearl
The Picture of Dorian Gray
Poems of W.B. Yeats: The Rose
Portrait of the Artist as a Young Man
Pride and Prejudice
Prometheus Bound
Pudd'nhead Wilson
Pygmalion
Rabbit, Run
A Raisin in the Sun
The Real Life of Sebastian Knight
Red Badge of Courage
The Republic
Richard II
Richard III
The Rime of the Ancient Mariner
Robinson Crusoe
Roll of Thunder, Hear My Cry
Romeo and Juliet
A Room of One's Own
A Room With a View
Rosencrantz and Guildenstern Are Dead
Salome

The Scarlet Letter
Secret Sharer
Sense and Sensibility
A Separate Peace
Shakespeare's Sonnets
Siddhartha
Silas Marner
Sir Gawain and the Green Knight
Sister Carrie
Six Characters in Search of an Author
Slaughterhouse Five
Snow Falling on Cedars
The Social Contract
Something Wicked This Way Comes
Song of Roland
Sons and Lovers
The Sorrows of Young Werther
The Sound and the Fury
Spring Awakening
The Stranger
A Streetcar Named Desire
The Sun Also Rises
Tale of Two Cities
The Taming of the Shrew
The Tempest
Tender is the Night
Tess of the D'Urbervilles
Their Eyes Were Watching God
Things Fall Apart
The Threepenny Opera

The Time Machine
Titus Andronicus
To Build a Fire
To Kill a Mockingbird
To the Lighthouse
Treasure Island
Troilus and Cressida
Turn of the Screw
Twelfth Night
Ulysses
Uncle Tom's Cabin
Utopia
A Very Old Man With Enormous Wings
The Visit
Volpone
Waiting for Godot
Waiting for Lefty
Walden
Washington Square
Where the Red Fern Grows
White Fang
White Noise
White Teeth
Who's Afraid of Virginia Woolf
Winesburg, Ohio
The Winter's Tale
Woyzeck
Wuthering Heights
The Yellow Wallpaper
Yonnondio: From the Thirties

For our full list of over 250 Study Guides, Quizzes,
Sample College Application Essays, Literature Essays and E-texts, visit:

**www.gradesaver.com**

Made in the USA